INVITED

Invited

THE CALL *of* A LIFETIME

Roger Wernette

Whitecaps Media
Houston

Whitecaps Media
Houston, Texas
whitecapsmedia.com

Invited: The Call of a Lifetime
© 2014 by Roger Wernette
All rights reserved

ISBN: 978-0-9883628-8-8

Printed in the United States of America

To contact Roger Wernette to speak to your group or for information on bulk sales, please visit our website or email us at ran@whitecapsmedia.com

CONTENTS

1. An Interesting Call   7

2. The Invitation   16

3. Who Is Doing the Inviting?   26

4. So What Is the Kingdom of God?   34

5. Isn't This Really Just about
   Going to Heaven or Hell?   43

6. Wait … There Is a Huge Problem   49

7. The Root of the Issue   58

8. The Sacrifice for Sin   68

9. Eyewitnesses   78

10. The Loophole   89

11. Scared Men Changing the World   101

12. The Invitation Revisited   111

13. Invited to Know Life   119

     Discussion Questions   127

     How to Use This Book   134

     For Further Reading   136

CHAPTER 1

An Interesting Call

Let's play a game of make-believe. When I was a kid, we started many conversations with the words, "Let's play like ..." Humor me for a moment. Plus, what choice do you have? You really can't quit reading this book in the first paragraph, can you?

Play like it is a Saturday afternoon and you are just settling in to watch your favorite college team play football. You are ready to relax and watch someone else take a beating for a change. You might already be getting drowsy. This is going to be a nice day.

Suddenly, the phone rings and after a couple of rings, you decide to go ahead and answer. The Caller ID says "Restricted" so you can't tell who is calling. The operator on the other end says, "Please hold for the governor of the state." You are somewhat interested but you suspect that this is a trick or, at best, a recorded message. While still watching the game, you listen to the call. Maybe you glance out the window to see if some of your friends are out there playing what seems to be an obvious joke on you.

When the next voice comes on, you realize that this might not be a spoof. You think you recognize the voice of the *real* governor say, "Roger, how are you? It's good to talk to you. You may be wondering why I'm calling. I want to meet you and get to know you, and I want you to get to know me as well. I would like for you to work with me and help me in an important service to our citizens. You have a special skill set, and I have a position that fits you perfectly. Our state needs a person like you. You can become a great person of influence from this position, and we will help equip you to do the job. Would you be interested in meeting with me right away?"

Now you are wide awake. You no longer care if you voted for this person or if you agree with any or all of your state's policies. All you know is that you are talking to the leader of your state, and he called *you*. What does this call say about you? You must have characteristics and talents that you did not know you had. Maybe you are really important and didn't even know it! You are engaged and ready. If this is a real offer, you are definitely going to check it out.

"I can be ready whenever you need me." The words have come flying out of your mouth.

You cannot wait to get to that meeting! This is a chance to serve the people of your state, but more than that, it is an opportunity to work with an influential leader who picked *you* as a partner. It may be a chance to influence history! This will most likely cause a significant change in your own life.

"OK, my assistant Marge will come on and set up the details. All you have to do is be ready. I will fly in from the capital and will pick you up at your house. I will personally brief you as we travel. We have already run your security clearance and you passed. I will see you on Thursday morning. Thanks for your help."

The phone goes into hold mode and after a few seconds, Marge comes on and informs you that the governor will be at your home on Thursday at 9 A.M., just as you were previously told. Marge already has your address. She tells you what to bring and to pack enough clothes to last three days. She has no other information for you. The rest will be conveyed to you personally by the governor during the meetings you two will have. As she gets ready to hang up, she casually asks you how your spouse is (called specifically by name) and mentions that you ought to be proud of your son's straight "A" report card that he got last month. She hopes that she can meet them soon. As quickly as the call began, it is now over and the dial tone notifies you of this fact.

The football game is forgotten. You now go back over the conversation. What if this was a hoax? You check your email and sure enough, a confirmation has already arrived, along with a note from Marge. The email address, of course, ends with ".gov". The phone number, which you are urged to call if you have any questions matches the capital area code. You are now ready for a trip, but there are several things that you don't know.

No one mentioned *where* you were going. You first assumed that the capital would be your destination, but since you are being picked up, you really don't know. The details of your meeting with the governor were totally left out. You don't know *why* you are going. You know that the governor will be accompanying you, but you don't know *who* else will attend. And you have no idea as to *what* you will be doing. But who cares? This is the governor, a national figure. You've seen him on CNN, for heaven's sake! You cannot miss this chance!

If the story above happened to any of us, we would react just like "you" reacted to the invitation. The call was not to go *to* some place. You were simply invited to meet with the governor. The location was irrelevant. If it were at the local coffee shop, you would still go. The job that you would do is not that important. You will do whatever the governor wants you to do. It is a once in a lifetime call and you don't want to miss it. Who knows what will come out of this? Your whole life will probably be changed. No one would turn down an opportunity like this. You will get to know the governor! You must go. You are compelled to go. Who wouldn't go?

Now let's change the story up, just a little. It's the same scene. It's the same football game and the same day. The phone call is different, however. This time the voice on the phone says, "Please hold for the Creator of the Universe." This is the One who *created the governor*. The contents of the call are very similar to the previous one.

"Roger, this is God. I am calling you to invite you to be a part of something great. I want you to know Me and to be a part of My world. I created you with a great set of gifts and talents that I want to use for My purposes. I will give you all the tools and energy that you need. All you have to do is follow along. I would like to meet with you so I can tell you what I want you to do. I have made special arrangements in order for us to get together. This is going to be a fantastic assignment that will change your life. When can you meet?"

Miraculously, here is your response: "Well, God, I am pretty busy today. Next week doesn't seem possible, either, since I have to go to Seattle and meet with a client. Our kids are graduating from high school and grade school this spring and we just don't have much time. My wife has been on edge lately because of her job and she is keeping me up late at night because she needs to talk. My work is just awful and I am there nearly ten hours a day. This is just such a tough stretch for me. Could we visit some other time?"

Who in the world would have such a reply to this invitation? The answer is that almost *all* of us have replied to God like that. Isn't it interesting? Why would we jump if someone "really important" called us and asked us for a meeting, but when God calls, we put Him off?

There are a couple of reasons why we might react in this way. First, it has been pounded into our head that a life with God is all about "church" stuff. You know ... being good, getting sent to Africa as a missionary, having to attend church every Sunday, giving all your money away, and otherwise missing out on the real fun. We only get one life and why should we spend it just trying to be good? Why not really enjoy life? Didn't someone say, "Eat, drink, and be merry, because tomorrow we may die?" Besides, who wants to be good just so we can go to heaven and fly around with little wings and play a harp?

Secondly, we have a misunderstanding about God's intentions. We do not realize that He is offering us a relationship and a chance to get to know Him. We don't understand that God's call is an invitation to experience His presence and to know how each of us fits into His kingdom. It is about coming to first know Him and secondly, to know why He created us.

Most of us love to imagine ourselves knowing important people. We like to meet celebrities and get their autographs. We follow famous people on Twitter and sometimes send them a tweet, hoping to get a reply. If that should happen, we wind it into every conversation. We received a Twitter message directly from our favorite baseball star. How exciting! And if the governor called us, we would bring it up every chance we got. No matter what question we were asked, we would mention the governor.

If someone said, "Pass the potatoes," our answer would be, "You know, the governor loves potatoes. Did I tell you that I had lunch with the governor just the other day? I am on a big state project. Yep, I was with the governor last week. A real nice person, the governor. A good friend of mine."

We love to be important and to be viewed as someone with influence and power. A meeting with the top official of our state might make you feel special, but what if you got the chance to meet the Creator of the World? What if He offered you *His* friendship? The chance to be in His presence and to glimpse into the mind of God would be an astounding offer. And what if that Presence could actually transform you? If you could know God maybe you could know why He created you. You could understand what your purpose is and what you are really supposed to be doing. To know God would unlock mysteries about your life and the universe. If that was possible, there is *no one* who shouldn't be interested.

Jesus said, "I am the way, the truth, and the life" (John 14:6).

What if we were invited to know the way to life? What if there is a real purpose to your life that goes far beyond just living until you die? What if life is not just "play like," but a one-and-only chance to be all you can be? Wouldn't that opportunity to know God prompt you to read a short book and ask some questions?

My hope is that you will make yourself available for a brief look at an invitation that will forever change your life. We will begin by looking at an ancient conversation in which a group of unlikely candidates were asked a very unlikely question.

CHAPTER 2

The Invitation

A plain and simple invitation. Very understandable and straightforward. Two thousand years ago, a man named Jesus came walking down the shoreline. Two fishermen named Simon and Andrew were casting a net out into the lake. Just a couple of guys doing some fishing. Jesus invited them to come and follow Him. As a part of that invitation, He said He would make something special out of them. He would show them how their lives could really count. How did these guys react? They immediately left all of their fishing equipment and followed Him. The nets, the boat, and whatever else they had with them were forgotten as they accepted Jesus' invitation. Here's how the Bible tells the story:

> Passing alongside the Sea of Galilee, he saw Simon and Andrew the brother of Simon casting a net into the sea, for they were fishermen. And Jesus said to them, "Follow me,

and I will make you become fishers of men."
And immediately they left their nets and followed him.

—MARK 1:16–18

Now read as almost the exact same scene
is repeated with two more fishermen, James
and John. Not only did they answer this call of
Jesus and leave their possessions, they also left
their father sitting in the boat! And they did it
"immediately":

And going on a little farther, he saw James
the son of Zebedee and John his brother,
who were in their boat mending the nets.
And immediately he called them, and they
left their father Zebedee in the boat with the
hired servants and followed him.

—MARK 1:19–20

What caused these men to move so quickly?
This must have been an unexpected offer. It
meant more to them than their work, evidenced
by the deserted boats, gear, and loved ones.
These accounts would lead one to believe that
these guys wanted something new in their lives.
This call of Jesus apparently touched them in
such a way that they could not resist following

this Man. They seemed to pursue Jesus as if they had been waiting their entire lives for Him to come along and invite them on this mysterious trip.

Some biblical scholars believe that these young men were fishing because they may have been turned down for another career. To young Jewish boys of the time, discipleship with a local rabbi was a great aspiration. The rabbi would interview candidates to be his disciples and to follow him. He would test their biblical knowledge and then take only the "best of the best." Those that were simply "good" were not acceptable. It took an exceptional candidate to attract the attention of a rabbi—only the outstanding young men were invited to follow him.

Those turned down as potential disciples could only go and seek employment. If their family had a business, the rabbi may have directed them to participate in that career since they were not qualified to follow him. Thus, it would not be surprising if this were the story of these fishermen. If this were the case, fishing may have been a poor substitute for what they really wanted to do. Day after day the mundane duties of mending and cleaning nets would wear on anyone. The smelly chore of sorting and cleaning fish would get old. The task was always there, waiting for them to drag themselves out of their homes early every morning just to catch a few fish. Was this all there was to life?

Some of us ask ourselves the same question. Countless men and women rise early each day in order to report to jobs they don't like in order to perform duties handed out by arrogant and difficult superiors who treat them badly. If only there was a way to see the real purpose in life. Will our whole life be just a series of sales calls? Will we fidget over spreadsheets forever?

Many young people go to school day in and day out without seeing a purpose for their education. They watch their friends go down the tube for drugs, sex, and alcohol, with some actually losing their lives due to overdose. Many are missing the thrill of real life in exchange for some momentary euphoria. It just doesn't seem to make sense.

So into the world of these fishermen, Jesus came asking. Here was a real offer: to be more than they ever imagined. For them, it was their chance to do something greater than just fish. Jesus offered to make them fishers of men! What could that mean? Could He possibly change them into men whose lives really counted? What if life could be better?

The offer of Jesus sounded like an invitation to a business deal. "*You* come follow me, and *I* will transform your life into one that has meaning." They were invited to be disciples of this man Jesus who told them that they could be in the people-catching business. The agreement was that the disciples would follow and thereby Jesus would transform them. Jesus posed His question in their terms. "I will make you fishers of men." For us, He might say, "Come follow Me and I will transform you into the person you were created to be. Through a friendship with Me, I will show you what life is really supposed to be."

What did it mean to follow Jesus? It meant that He would lead them to do what He did. They would go where He went and become known as His disciples. A student becomes like his teacher. An athlete takes up the technique and philosophy of his coach. A dancer imitates the moves of her instructor. The fishermen were invited to move around the world with Jesus and become identified with Him.

What would that life look like? They would soon discover this. If you read Mark 1:21–39 from the Bible, you can see what Jesus did. Here is the first part:

And they went into Capernaum, and immediately on the Sabbath he entered the synagogue and was teaching. And they were astonished at his teaching, for he taught them as one who had authority, and not as the scribes. And immediately there was in their synagogue a man with an unclean spirit. And he cried out, "What have you to do with us, Jesus of Nazareth? Have you come to destroy us? I know who you are— the Holy One of God." But Jesus rebuked him, saying, "Be silent, and come out of him!" And the unclean spirit, convulsing him and crying out with a loud voice, came out of him. And they were all amazed, so that they questioned among themselves, saying, "What is this? A new teaching with authority! He commands even the unclean spirits, and they obey him." And at once his fame spread everywhere throughout all the surrounding region of Galilee.

—MARK 1:21–28

He first went into the synagogue and began teaching. The Bible says that people were astonished when they heard Him teach. They had never heard anyone say the things that Jesus said about God. While He was teaching, a man came in and interrupted Him. The Bible says that this man had an "unclean" spirit. We might say that he was crazy. He fell down in front of Jesus and said, "What have you to do with us, Jesus of Nazareth? Have you come to destroy us? I know who you are—the Holy One of God." This wild man recognized Him! He said what many people say today, "I know all about Jesus, and He just wants to wreck my life."

The man in the story then fell down in front of Jesus and started convulsing! OK, I haven't seen many people do that. The fishermen who followed Jesus must have had their mouths hanging wide open. They probably could not believe it. And then Jesus said, "Be silent, and come out of him!" Then the man became quiet. The new disciples probably now understood this would be no ordinary life. The news about Jesus spread far and wide!

> And immediately he left the synagogue and entered the house of Simon and Andrew, with James and John. Now Simon's mother-in-law lay ill with a fever, and immediately they told him about her. And he came and took her by the hand and lifted her up, and the fever left her, and she began to serve them.
>
> That evening at sundown they brought to him all who were sick or oppressed by

demons. And the whole city was gathered
together at the door. And he healed many
who were sick with various diseases, and
cast out many demons. And he would not
permit the demons to speak, because they
knew him.

—MARK 1:29–34

Jesus then went to Simon's house (one of
the fishermen) and saw that his mother-in-law
was sick. So He healed her. The little group of
fishermen may have never seen someone care
like Jesus, who was concerned for people in all
circumstances!

That night Simon (who was later called
Peter) may have looked out the window and
seen *the whole town* gathered outside his house.
What a shock! Everyone who lived in the vicin-
ity was gathered at his home waiting for Jesus to
heal them! Jesus stayed up late healing people,
spending a great deal of time and energy caring
for them.

That is not all He did that caught the attention of His new disciples:

And rising very early in the morning, while
it was still dark, he departed and went out
to a desolate place, and there he prayed.

And Simon and those who were with him searched for him, and they found him and said to him, "Everyone is looking for you." And he said to them, "Let us go on to the next towns, that I may preach there also, for that is why I came out." And he went throughout all Galilee, preaching in their synagogues and casting out demons.

—MARK 1:35–39

Jesus got up the next day before sunrise just to go pray. (I don't know about you, but after doing all those miracles, I would have slept in!) His followers went looking for Him. There were probably now others who wanted to be healed. The fishermen couldn't believe that Jesus was out alone while so many people still needed help. When they told Jesus that everyone was looking for Him (for more miracles), He said He needed to go preach in other places.

How did Jesus know that He should go elsewhere? He seemed to have a plan for His life, and one for them as well. Jesus had the same kind of relationship with God that He was offering these people with Himself. He had been talking to God since before the sun came up. Jesus had been thinking and praying with the Creator of the world about what came next in His life. Following

Jesus was going to be more than just a religious experience. It would be an adventure with One who seemed to know the mind of God.

How could Jesus perform these healings? How could He promise to change the lives of the fishermen? Jesus was not a known religious leader. He was not a rabbi at the local synagogue. His vocation had, up until now, been carpentry and construction. Was He making promises that He could not keep? What right did He have to offer the position of "fishers of men" to them? What was His authority?

In the next chapter we will discuss who Jesus was and how He could make this incredible offer.

CHAPTER 3

Who Is Doing the Inviting?

If a stranger came up to you and offered you a job, what would you want to know first? No, not how many days of vacation you would get. You wouldn't first want to know if the position came with a car (although that question might come later). Even the amount of salary would be a secondary issue. You would *first* need to be sure that this person had the authority to offer said employment. I could personally offer you a great job at the biggest company in the world, along with a top salary. There is just one problem: I do not possess the right to hand out jobs at that company. I don't even work there. I have no authority to make such a proposal.

In the previous chapter, we saw Jesus making an unbelievable statement to the four fishermen. He told them that He could make them into something special. He invited them to come along with Him and He would transform them. "Follow Me and *I will make you ...*" Jesus had been preaching that He had brought the kingdom of God into the world, and we can assume that He was inviting them to come with Him into that kingdom. Unless you believe that the world just happened by accident (and some do), you should be interested in an invitation to this kingdom of God. It would be an opportunity to know the Creator of the world.

But wait ... what gave Jesus the authority to make such an offer? Take a look at the way the book of John begins:

> In the beginning was the Word, and the Word was with God, and the Word was God. He was in the beginning with God. All things were made through him, and without him was not any thing made that was made. In him was life, and the life was the light of men.
>
> —JOHN 1:1–4

There is a very good chance that you have seen this passage before. It says that in the beginning was the Word and that this Word was *with* God, and, even more, that this Word *was* God! The passage says that "He" was with God in the beginning. The Word was a person and this person was God. As you read on, you see that through this Word, all things were created. According to the Bible, the Word created everything, and nothing was created without Him. And finally it says that in this Word was life. So life came from the Word and no life came from any other source. The Word was the one and only Creator. Now watch this:

> And the Word became flesh and dwelt among us, and we have seen his glory, glory as of the only Son from the Father, full of grace and truth ... No one has ever seen God; the only God, who is at the Father's side, he has made him known.
>
> —JOHN 1:14, 18

John's Gospel now says that the Word became flesh (became a man) and made His dwelling among us. This Word came and lived among us. If the Word was God (remember?), this means that God came and lived on earth. The apostle John says that "we have seen Him" (not just "I" saw Him, but that "we" saw Him). There were others who believed like John and they saw Him also. From verse 14 of John 1, we come to see that John 1:1–3 is saying that the "One and Only Son" was the Word. The Word was in the beginning with God and actually was God. John believed that He had seen God embodied as a man!

Who was that man? John the Baptist once pointed Him out as "the Lamb of God" (John 1:29). John the apostle (who wrote the Gospel of John) is telling us that the man was Jesus. Jesus was the Word become flesh. He was God on earth, existing as the One and Only Son. The Creator of the Universe came and walked on earth and brought grace and truth to His creation, man.

The Bible goes on to describe more about God's existence on earth. There is a neat word picture in the original Greek of John's writing. The word translated "dwelt" actually means "tabernacled" or "pitched a tent" or "camped." John hung around Jesus for three years and watched Him closely as He performed many miracles. This disciple was saying that the God of the universe came down and pitched His tent among mere mortal men! He walked with people and lived with them. God ate with them. He laughed with them and cried with them. Jesus felt all the things that men and women feel as they live. John, having lived with Jesus, believed that Jesus was God who had come to live on earth!

Have you ever gone camping with someone? You get to know them really well. A number of years ago, as a Young Life leader, I took high school kids to camps and sometimes we would go out on the hiking trail with them. We got to know them. We heard their stories. By hanging out with them, we found out who they really were. We could not have known them like we did just by passing them in the hall or by going to a sporting event. We had to go "live with them" for a while (about a week was all we could take!). Not only did we get to know them, they got to know us.

Here is some really great news … the God of the universe truly knows you. What's more, He offers you the chance to know Him. He created you. He has lived on earth. He came and hung out. There is no other story like this. It is one that you could *not* make up. It is the story of God who chose to reveal Himself to mankind *as a man*. That's what I call creativity.

If you were God, how would you choose to communicate with your created people? If it were me, I might skywrite some messages. Or maybe I would throw down some flyers from heaven. I might even plan a visit. I might come down a golden escalator and have bands playing. I would descend grandly and wave. I would meet with some folks, probably the important world leaders. I could tell them all about me and what I had in mind when I created them.

But there is one thing I would not do. I wouldn't stay. At the end of the day or weekend or week, I would get back on the escalator and ride back home. I would tell everyone, "Good luck!" and say, "I'll call you," or, "Maybe we can get lunch." But I would always go back. The thought of living on this earth would be revolting to me. I wouldn't want to "get dirty."

God didn't do that. He stayed. We will see later just how far He took it. But by living on earth instead of remaining in heaven, He did something that I would never do. I would never lower myself to spend time with people who would eventually reject me.

God was willing to subject Himself to our scrutiny for the sole reason of offering His ongoing relationship with us. If God did this, shouldn't we at least check out the story? To many, it just seems so implausible. That was even the case with some of His closest friends.

Near the end of His life, Jesus had this exchange with Philip, one of His disciples:

> Philip said to him, "Lord, show us the Father, and it is enough for us." Jesus said to him, "Have I been with you so long, and you still do not know me, Philip? Whoever has seen me has seen the Father. How can you say, 'Show us the Father'? Do you not

believe that I am in the Father and the Father is in me? The words that I say to you I do not speak on my own authority, but the Father who dwells in me does his works. Believe me that I am in the Father and the Father is in me, or else believe on account of the works themselves.

—JOHN 14:8–11

If you have trouble believing that Jesus was God come to earth, you are not alone. Even His disciples, the guys with whom He spent most of His time, could not quite understand it. Philip said that if Jesus could just show them the Father (God) that would be enough. God spoke back to him and said, "Don't you know Me, Philip?" God had been living with them the whole time. Jesus pointed out that the words He gave them came straight from God. And if that was impossible to believe, Philip only needed to look at the miracles Jesus performed.

Time and time again, Jesus revealed His godliness by healing the sick. He calmed the waters. He turned other water into wine. He read peoples' minds. He touched lepers (no one would do that). He befriended those whom no one wanted. He hung out with liars, winos, prostitutes, and cheaters. He loved children and they loved Him.

His entire life was a miracle that was witnessed by hundreds of people. His story is better documented than any other person's in ancient history. It was not made up. It happened as surely as Napoleon stormed Europe and Alexander the Great took over the world. There is no doubt that Jesus lived. It is a fact of history.

Keep working through the Bible and you will see that all of the writing agrees. Jesus was God. And He was not the kind of God that I would be. He did not try to be superior to those with whom He pitched His tent. He became a servant! The God of the universe not only performed miracles, He also washed feet (see John 13). And eventually, Jesus died a death that no one else would dream to die. He did it all to communicate His essence. His love. His Word. This Word, this Communication, this Revelation, is a loving God who created us to be a part of His kingdom.

That is the authority by which Jesus can make any invitation that He wants. He is God. He has all the authority He needs because He is the Creator. Your Creator. My Creator. No one knows you like God. It was He who invited those fishermen to follow Him, and it is He who now invites you to do the same.

CHAPTER 4

So What Is the Kingdom of God?

Jesus' invitation to the fishermen that day by the lake was to follow Him. It was also an offer to come into the kingdom of God. It is not every day that one gets invited into a kingdom. The Jewish people had waited thousands of years for this new kingdom. They had been oppressed by the Persians, Syrians, and Babylonians, just to mention a few. Now the Romans had invaded their land, and they were looking for the new kingdom promised to them in the Old Testament book of Daniel.

> And in the days of those kings the God of heaven will set up a kingdom that shall never be destroyed, nor shall the kingdom be left to another people. It shall break in pieces all these kingdoms and bring them to an end, and it shall stand forever.
>
> —DANIEL 2:44

When John the Baptist appeared with his prophecy, the people came in droves to hear him talk about this new kingdom. Most of them assumed that it would be a political kingdom that would free them from the oppressive Romans. Naturally, they were excited.

> John appeared, baptizing in the wilderness and proclaiming a baptism of repentance for the forgiveness of sins. And all the country of Judea and all Jerusalem were going out to him and were being baptized by him in the river Jordan, confessing their sins. Now John was clothed with camel's hair and wore a leather belt around his waist and ate locusts and wild honey. And he preached, saying, "After me comes he who is mightier than I, the strap of whose sandals I am not worthy to stoop down and untie. I have baptized you with water, but he will baptize you with the Holy Spirit."
>
> —MARK 1:4–8

This kingdom was different from what the people expected. The Jews were expecting God to help them overcome the Romans. They were waiting for their powerful God to exhibit His strength on earth and to free them literally from their oppressors. The Messiah they had looked for would give them peace on earth (like we sing about at Christmas time). What a day that would be!

Many people today are a lot like those who inhabited Israel at the time of John. Some believe Jesus has just come to make them rich and comfortable. They might think God's job is to make life easy. This is a grave misconception. Jesus came to bring the kingdom of God to man so that man could understand the greatness of life as it was meant to be. It is more about transformation and change than it is about ease and comfort.

A deeper look at what was offered to them by John the Baptist, and later by Jesus, shows that it was not the political and earthly freedom they wanted. This kingdom required them to repent. The word "repent" actually means to stop and turn around, to do something new and different. This requires people to look inside themselves and see that things need to be different. But the Jewish people thought it was *their environment* that was going to change; not *them*. The Romans were the ones who needed to repent. John seemed to be saying that *they* should repent. What kind of kingdom was this?

And what about the guy who came announcing the kingdom? John the Baptist was a wild man. He lived in the desert. He dressed in camel's hair (and not one of those sport coats) and ate locusts and wild honey. There is little wonder why the people had such a hard time understanding that this new kingdom would be heralded by a man who lived alone in the wilderness, dressed in animal skins, and ate bugs. How would you like him to direct your retirement investments?

Then, a carpenter from Nazareth, named Jesus, continued the Kingdom proclamation:

> Now after John was arrested, Jesus came into Galilee, proclaiming the gospel of God, and saying, "The time is fulfilled, and the kingdom of God is at hand; repent and believe in the gospel."
>
> —MARK 1:14–15

What kind of kingdom would be led by a construction worker? He might know a lot about wood and how to build things, but surely He did not understand revolutions and changing the world? Not only that, but Jesus had grown up in the same area where He now began to teach. Imagine one of the children in your neighborhood who, later in life, came home and began to talk about a new world order. You might say,

"This is the kid who used to rake my yard. Who is he to talk like this?"

Jesus said the time had come and the kingdom of God was near. The years of waiting had ended for the people of God. God had now stepped onto the earth and was in the process of changing the world to prepare it for His rule. What did "the kingdom is near" mean? It meant that it was available to God's people; to those who accepted the invitation to follow Jesus. The kingdom had come to the people in the form of Jesus, and now the dominion of God was going to impact the world.

But isn't the kingdom of God just about church and always trying to be good? And isn't church just about praying and singing and pretending to be good? Who wants to go through life trying to live up to God's report card? What fun! Yet when one looks at where Jesus went and what He did, the kingdom of God seems more like a party than a way to act holy.

Take a look at this:

On the third day there was a wedding at Cana in Galilee, and the mother of Jesus was there. Jesus also was invited to the wedding with his disciples. When the wine ran out, the mother of Jesus said to him, "They have no wine." And Jesus said to her, "Woman, what does this have to do with me? My hour has not yet come." His mother said to the servants, "Do whatever he tells you."

Now there were six stone water jars there for the Jewish rites of purification, each holding twenty or thirty gallons. Jesus said to the servants, "Fill the jars with water." And they filled them up to the brim. And he said to them, "Now draw some out and take it to the master of the feast." So they took it. When the master of the feast tasted the water now become wine, and did not know where it came from (though the servants who had drawn the water knew), the master of the feast called the bridegroom and said to him, "Everyone serves the good wine first, and when people have drunk freely, then the poor wine. But you have kept the good wine until now."

—JOHN 2:1–10

It is interesting that Jesus was at this wedding. Many think that Jesus was just a cosmic killjoy who came to earth to make life miserable. But who do you invite to your wedding, anyway? You want the people that you like the most and the ones who will add to the occasion.

No one would deliberately invite some dud who would ruin the party. And here was Jesus at the party as an invited guest. On the most important day of their lives, the bride and groom must have thought that Jesus should be there.

Then something really serious happened. They ran out of wine! That could absolutely kill a wedding, especially when the water of the day was nasty and untreated. Imagine all of the great food that is served at a wedding, accompanied by a brown glass of water that would eventually make everyone sick. They needed wine to make the occasion special.

Jesus' mother took charge and told the servants to do whatever He said. She knew that He cared and had the ability to fix the situation. While she may not have known what Jesus would do, she trusted that He loved the wedding couple. He would come up with something. Even when Jesus mildly protested, saying that it was not a time to involve Him, His mom instructed the servants to do whatever He said.

So He told them to fill ceremonial washing jars with water—the regular, brown water. Yep, they put it in vessels reserved for washing. If you were a servant, you may have thought this was not going to end well. Then, and get this, He told them to draw the water out and serve it to the person in charge of the party. The servants probably thought that they would be fired (at best). They were going to ask the master of ceremonies to drink the bad water out of a jar in which people washed their hands!

When the master of the banquet tasted the bad water, he had the servants killed. Then they called off the wedding and everyone went home. No, I'm just kidding. When they brought the water to him, it had been changed into the greatest wine that he had ever tasted! The party was a success!

Many people believe that Jesus will not help them enjoy life. They think He will make them do things they don't want to do. Like become a missionary or smile at strangers on the bus. But that is not the Jesus the Bible describes. He may call us to be missionaries and may even call you to love strangers, but it is much greater than that. This Jesus cares about enjoying life. He would be the One you would invite to your party. If He were physically here today, people would want to be with Him. He might be the One telling stories and laughing with everyone. He would see life as a great celebration. Tony Campolo once wrote a book called *The Kingdom of God is a Party*. In it, he said that God celebrates when men and women become the followers of Jesus.

We are talking about a God who rejoices in the life He created, and He wants others to do the same. Campolo was right; the kingdom of God *is* supposed to be a party.

The great news is that the kingdom of God is not just about trying to be good. It is a constant celebration of who God is and who you as a new creation can become. It is about being made free to know God and getting to know the real you. When you begin to learn from Jesus and *to follow* Him, you start to discover your worth, but even more, you discover God's place in your life. The kingdom of God truly is a joyous experience because it is in that Kingdom that we come to know our Creator. And you are invited to join in on the celebration.

CHAPTER 5

Isn't This Really Just about Going to Heaven or Hell?

When I was about ten years old, my pastor told us at vacation Bible school that if we didn't want to go to hell, we should come down to the front of the church and accept Jesus into our heart. I shot down there because I, for one, did not want to go to hell. It seemed to me that heaven would be much more comfortable than hell. I mean, who wants to go through eternity without central air conditioning?

So I took Jesus into my heart as my pastor had invited me to do. I wasn't totally sure what that meant, but apparently now I didn't have to worry about going to hell. Once I had made the decision to have Jesus as my Savior, I had my ticket punched to an everlasting life of comfort.

And from then on, if someone asked me to raise my hand to reaffirm my belief in Jesus, I did it. I didn't want there to be any question of where I would spend eternity.

The problem was that I had not made the same decision that Simon, Andrew, James, and John made when they decided to *follow* Jesus that day beside the lake (you read about it in chapter 2 ... remember?). No one told me about that. My pastor forgot to mention that following Jesus was a conscious decision that someone makes when they "go down front" or when they "accept Jesus into their heart."

Is the call of God really just about heaven and hell? Is God simply issuing us a "get out of hell free" card?

Coming to Jesus is *not* simply a matter of choosing a *destination*. If you remember in my initial illustration of the governor calling, your destination was never stated. The governor invited you to meet him and he was going to pick you up. You did not ask where he was taking you. The major issue was that you were going to get to be with the governor. You would get to meet him and hear his ideas. He was going to share with you a vision, and he wanted you to be a part of that. You were flattered and encouraged that he thought enough of you to come and meet with you. All of a sudden, you had worth. Your old sense of inadequacy was gone. The governor's interest in you had changed the game.

The same goes for heaven. Why would I want to go there? Certainly, if you tell me that I may be punished eternally if I go to hell, I may listen to you. The very thought of a hell might be enough to get my attention. But there has to be more to eternity than just hot or cold, comfortable or miserable, bliss or punishment.

Following Jesus is more than finding a comfortable place to spend eternity. It is about coming to know and follow the Creator of the Universe. Jesus, as God on earth, came to invite us into His own presence. He wants us to be with Him. He wants it so much so that He was willing to live on this earth with us. We have been invited to know and enjoy fellowship with the Creator of all mankind! He came to earth to be with us and to allow us to know and be with Him.

Please don't get me wrong: I believe in heaven and in hell. I want to go to heaven! But the reason I want to go there is because that is where Jesus is. And after seeing in the Bible what Jesus did for me, I *really* want to be with Him. I want to go to heaven, not because it is a place without pain and suffering (and that *is* how the

Bible describes heaven). Not just because the city and streets are made of pure gold (and they *are*—read Revelation 21). I want to go there, not because the alternative place to go is hell (and it *is*). Heaven is where I want to be because Jesus is there. Jesus is the prize, not a destination!

Just to be sure that we understand each other: The Bible mentions hell as a real place. There is no question that hell exists. Below are just three passages in which hell is mentioned:

> "And if your hand causes you to sin, cut it off. It is better for you to enter life crippled than with two hands to go to hell, to the unquenchable fire. And if your foot causes you to sin, cut it off. It is better for you to enter life lame than with two feet to be thrown into hell. And if your eye causes you to sin, tear it out. It is better for you to enter the kingdom of God with one eye than with two eyes to be thrown into hell, 'where their worm does not die and the fire is not quenched.' "
>
> —MARK 9:43–48

He will punish those who do not know God and do not obey the gospel of our Lord Jesus. They will be punished with

everlasting destruction and shut out from
the presence of the Lord and from the maj-
esty of his power.

—2 THESSALONIANS 1:8–9 (NIV 1984)

"But I say to you that everyone who is angry
with his brother will be liable to judgment;
whoever insults his brother will be liable to
the council; and whoever says, 'You fool!'
will be liable to the hell of fire."

—MATTHEW 5:22

We cannot argue that the Bible describes
heaven and hell as real and eternal places. We
should discuss these locations with great respect.
God, through Jesus, offers us heaven as a won-
derful place to live eternally that is available to
those who follow Jesus.

Hell is a real place, reserved for those who
lived their lives in rebellion against God without experiencing the forgiveness of Jesus. Those
who spend eternity in hell will miss all of God's
lovingkindess. In fact, Scripture says they will
spend eternity suffering "the punishment of
eternal destruction away from the presence of
the Lord" (2 Thessalonians 1:9).

On earth, every good thing we have comes
from God (James 1:17). We have crops that are

produced when God causes it to rain. We see the great mountains, valleys, and oceans. We have friends and experience life with them. But what would it be like if we didn't have any of these blessings? What if we were banned from love and the beauty of God's creation? Eternally? I do not want that, not for even one second.

Heaven is also real. Our perfect experience of God's presence makes it heaven. There we will get to spend eternity, without interruption, enjoying the true beauty of all that God created. Yes, on earth we enjoy many of God's blessings, but in heaven, we will know them all *perfectly*. Also, there won't be war, famine, terrorism, or anything else that would disturb our vision of God. There won't even be politics to cause me to dislike my neighbor. All those in heaven will live in peace with each other and with God. Heaven is going to be a great place!

But in the story of Christianity, Jesus is the Prize. Heaven is the by-product of knowing and following Him. I want to go to heaven because I want to meet Jesus face-to-face. When I get there He will welcome me as one of His own. I will finally get to experience His love perfectly.

Why do I want to get to heaven? Because my friend Jesus lives there.

CHAPTER 6

Wait ... There Is a Huge Problem

Have you ever been to a house that is completely full of people? I mean packed out. There is nowhere to turn and you can barely move from room to room. If you went to a party like this, you would ask, "What is the occasion? Why is this house so full?" It may be a birthday party for a really popular person, or maybe it is because there is a really special guest. If you begin to search for the reason for this huge gathering, you might have to worm your way around until, there in the corner, you find your explanation. Surrounded by a large group stands one of the most popular people in town. Everyone listens to stories and tales from this "celebrity." Everyone wants to get next to the guest of honor, which leads to even more folks crowding in.

Who would be the person in your town that you could invite to fill up your home? A local sports star? A famous performer? Maybe it would be a rich businessman that folks want to meet. If you wanted a full house, you would slyly mention to your friends that they might want to swing by and meet the quarterback of the local pro football team.

Let me be honest here: When I was younger, there is one person I would never have expected of filling a house. Jesus. What about you? What if you called your friends and asked them to come over and spend an evening with Jesus? Do you think they would show up? Some folks might be afraid to come over and meet Him; I know that would have been true of some of my friends. Maybe they would think He would be boring or judgmental or too religious. They might be suspicious: maybe this is some kind of fundraiser. They might decline because they think it just wouldn't be a fun way to spend an evening. But in the Bible, there is a story that turns out *just the opposite.*

> And when he returned to Capernaum after some days, it was reported that he was at home. And many were gathered together, so that there was no more room, not even at the door. And he was preaching the word to them.
>
> —MARK 2:1–2

Jesus was speaking at a home in Capernaum. He was the special guest of someone who wanted Him to teach his friends. Jesus was so popular that when the townspeople heard He was speaking, they filled up the house. There were so many that maybe they all had to stand. They were probably flowing out of the front door. This house was crowded!

This scene might change your mind as to what kind of person Jesus was when He was on earth. People do not go to see those whom they do not like. They go to see interesting people. They go to see someone who has something to offer. Many today believe that Jesus is someone to avoid. But when Jesus was on earth, people *wanted* to be near Him. They packed into this house *because* of Him, not *despite* Him. And He was preaching to them! How many preachers do you know that could pack out a house just by giving a sermon? Now take a look:

> And they came, bringing to him a paralytic carried by four men. And when they could not get near him because of the crowd, they removed the roof above him, and when they had made an opening, they let down the bed on which the paralytic lay.
>
> —MARK 2:3–4

Onto the scene came four men carrying a pallet with a paralyzed man on it. These guys had heard stories about Jesus. They picked up their friend and carried him to this Man who had healed many people in the town. Jesus had quite a reputation, and these men wanted to see if He would help their buddy. They arrived at the house only to find a great crowd already there. A quick look would have shown them that there was no way to get near Jesus.

These guys were persistent, so they looked for another way. They climbed up on the roof (roofs in those days were like patios). There was no window or door up there. Since there was no opening to get in, they made one! They started to dig down through dried mud and tiles. As Jesus was teaching, maybe a few people heard a strange scraping noise. A little dust drifted down. More scraping. More dust came down. Now one could see the smallest ray of light coming through the roof! Maybe the owner of the house started to notice. More digging and a lot more dust. Now pieces of mud were falling and maybe a piece of tile. Jesus may have stopped and looked up. Did He smile a little as He saw a face peering down? Now a whole lot more digging. Large pieces of roof were falling. The owner must have been aghast. A huge hole had opened up!

The hole was now dark. Something was covering the space. It looked like a blanket. Now it started to come down, and now a face looked over its edge. There was someone on it! They were lowering a person down through the ceiling! Finally the pallet was on the floor and the man on it might have looked somewhat embarrassed. The owner might have thought, "Gee, if you had just knocked ..."

Now let's pick up the rest of the story in the Bible:

> And when Jesus saw their faith, he said to
> the paralytic, "Son, your sins are forgiven."
>
> —MARK 2:5

Now it's the four friends who are aghast. They must have wanted to say, "No, Jesus, it's his legs. Not his sins. His legs! Just heal his legs!"

How could Jesus make such a mistake? It did not look like the man needed religion or forgiveness. It was evident that he needed to be healed of some kind of paralysis. The man could not walk and Jesus was pronouncing forgiveness over him. Jesus had it all wrong.

Or did He?

The obvious issue was that the man could not walk. But maybe that was not the problem at all. Jesus' main concern seemed to be the man's spiritual life. He wanted the man to know that his sins were forgiven. Without even asking the man about his situation, Jesus forgave him of his sins. Forgiveness would be good news for anyone, but how was it that Jesus, this carpenter, could possibly say that the man's sins were forgiven? How could He do that? People were there who wanted to ask the same question:

> Now some of the scribes were sitting there, questioning in their hearts, "Why does this man speak like that? He is blaspheming! Who can forgive sins but God alone?" And immediately Jesus, perceiving in his spirit that they thus questioned within themselves, said to them, "Why do you question these things in your hearts? Which is easier, to say to the paralytic, 'Your sins are forgiven,' or to say, 'Rise, take up your bed and walk'? But that you may know that the Son of Man has authority on earth to forgive sins"—he said to the paralytic—"I say to you, rise, pick up your bed, and go home." And he rose and immediately picked up his bed and went out before them all, so that they were all amazed and glorified God, saying, "We never saw anything like this!"
>
> —MARK 2:6–12

The teachers and priests were outraged at Jesus' statement. Forgiving sins was God's business. The only person who can forgive is the person who was wronged. If a friend of mine punched me in the nose (some friend!), *I* am the only one who can forgive that person. *I* was the one who was struck. No one else can forgive my attacker. Either *I* do it or no one does. Likewise, only God can forgive our sins, since those sins were against Him. When we act contrary to the Bible, we sin against God. We are breaking *His* commands. Therefore, it is His prerogative to forgive us or not.

So when Jesus forgave the man's sins, the teachers of the law were furious. It would have been sheer blasphemy to do something that was reserved for God. That was certainly not the work of a carpenter and itinerant preacher. And not only that, but anyone could *say*, "Your sins are forgiven." So how could Jesus prove that He could forgive sins?

The Bible says that Jesus knew what was on the minds of the teachers (that's a minor miracle in itself—Jesus was reading their minds!). Jesus now turned to the man and told him to pick up his mat and walk, and the man did it. By doing something that only God could do—healing this man of his paralysis—Jesus also proved His authority to forgive the man's sins. The man was totally healed, both inside and out.

Many of us carry guilt around with us every day. For some, this is overwhelming and paralyzing. Others may not think about it much, but in the quiet times, it is there. Questions like "How could I have said that?" or "Why did I do that?" or "What is wrong with me?" We need to be released from our burden. No one wants to carry around a load of "would've's," "could've's," or "should've's."

In the movie, *The Mission*, Robert De Niro plays a conquistador who gives up his proud and warring life to become a missionary to a group of Indians in South America. As penance for his past sinful lifestyle, a priest directs him to carry around his heavy armor and weapons in a bag. He is told to go to an Indian village that sits above a large waterfall. He climbs up the falls with this incredible weight tied around his neck and shoulders, falling several times. He drags the bag around until he becomes weary of the sheer burden of it all. Finally, he encounters one of the Indian tribesmen, who takes a knife and cuts the bag off. So great was his relief, both physically and emotionally, that De Niro's character collapses in tears. He is released of the guilt that plagued him and is free to pursue the life that he now wants to live.

For so many, there is a paralyzing guilt that spawns anxiety, depression, and isolation. The sin in one's life causes embarrassment and makes one want to hide from the issue. Many churches do not want to talk about sin because they think it might keep people from attending. Why drag them down by telling congregants that they aren't perfect? Yet this sin is present whether it is discussed or not. It holds folks down like a lead weight.

Wouldn't you love to enjoy the life for which you were created? The truth is that the forgiveness that will spell freedom and relief is just as available to you in Jesus as it was to the paralyzed man who was lowered through the roof that day. The forgiveness of Jesus will allow you to follow Him with the same abandon that the fishermen experienced that day beside the lake.

CHAPTER 7

The Root of the Issue

The Revolutionary War was not just a friendly disagreement. It was a brutal and bloody rebellion. The two sides were diametrically opposed to the views of the other. There was no way for these enemies to coexist. A war was the only solution.

During that war, if two people from opposite sides of the conflict ran into each other, they might well start shooting at each other in an attempt to eradicate the other side. This is the way war is. It is a violent disagreement in which neither side can live with the views of the other. The Revolutionary War was a total break in philosophy that could not be rectified. A war had to be fought in order to prove who was most powerful and, therefore, whose way would be followed.

So it goes with man and God. Since the fall of Adam and Eve, man has chosen to make his own decisions without any regard to what God may want. The fact that God created him is of no interest to rebellious man. Adam and Eve chose to disobey God. In doing so, they cut themselves off from fellowship with God and, as the Bible relates, they cut *us* off as well. The two ways of thinking, man's way and God's way, started a war that had to be settled. Here's the story:

> Now the serpent was more crafty than any other beast of the field that the LORD God had made. He said to the woman, "Did God actually say, 'You shall not eat of any tree in the garden'?" And the woman said to the serpent, "We may eat of the fruit of the trees in the garden, but God said, 'You shall not eat of the fruit of the tree that is in the midst of the garden, neither shall you touch it, lest you die.' " But the serpent said to the woman, "You will not surely die. For God knows that when you eat of it your eyes will be opened, and you will be like God, knowing good and evil."
>
> —GENESIS 3:1–5

Satan told Eve two lies as he presented Eve his proposition. First, he asked her if God had really prohibited Adam and Eve from eating *any* fruit from *any* tree in the garden. Isn't that like what we hear in the world? It is not uncommon for someone to say, "God doesn't want people to have any fun. He just wants to get His way and if you don't agree with Him, He smokes you."

These thoughts could not have been further from the truth in the garden, and Eve knew it. She told Satan, masquerading as a serpent, she could eat from any tree except one. God had created a beautiful and fruitful home for His creations. The entire garden was open to Adam and Eve. But they had to do it God's way. He created one tree that was off limits. They had to obey God and avoid this one tree. At issue was who they would follow and obey—themselves or God? To disobey God would mean certain death for Adam and Eve as they would be going against the Creator and Author of life. To rebel against God would be to turn against the life that He created. The first part of man's rebellion, therefore, is to disobey God.

Satan understood this so he gave Eve his second lie. He told her she would not die and that God's real motive was that He did not want anyone to know all He knew. At stake, according to Satan, was who would be God. If Eve knew everything that God knew, she could be like God. She could be her own god! Who then would need God? Eve could make up her own rules. This is the second part of man's war against God. Man wants to be God. He wants to be in control. God, however, communicates to man that there is only one God—and the position is already filled.

Isn't that the struggle that we all face? We do not like to be told what to do. When I was young, my favorite thing to tell my sisters was, "Don't tell me what to do! You aren't the boss of me." Many of us have avoided God because we are afraid of what He might tell us to do. We want to be able to make our own decisions. We want to be our own god.

The story goes on ...

> So when the woman saw that the tree was good for food, and that it was a delight to the eyes, and that the tree was to be desired to make one wise, she took of its fruit and ate, and she also gave some to her husband who was with her, and he ate. Then the eyes of both were opened, and they knew that they were naked. And they sewed fig leaves together and made themselves loincloths.
>
> —GENESIS 3:6–7

God had warned Adam and Eve that they would die if they ate from the tree, and while they did not die immediately after eating, they began to experience the slow march to death that we all do. They also died spiritually in that they were now separated from God by their sin. The relationship they had once enjoyed with the Creator of Life was shattered. And finally, they sentenced themselves to an eternal death, because their broken relationship with God could not be repaired by normal means.

Another result of their sin was that their eyes *were* opened and they *did* come to know things that only God had known up until then. For one, they realized they were naked. All the embarrassment and worries that are common-place in our lives came to them at once. They had to get dressed for the first time. Since shopping malls hadn't yet been invented, they had to make their own clothes. But clothes hadn't been invented either, so they got some fig leaves and made some makeshift coverings.

Also, up to that point they hadn't known the shame that comes from making major life errors. They hid from God in much the same way we avoid God. Not only were they embarrassed by each other, they were ashamed to be seen by God. So they hid from Him. How could they hide from the One who created them? Good question, isn't it? God, fully knowing where they were, called out to them:

And they heard the sound of the LORD God walking in the garden in the cool of the day, and the man and his wife hid themselves from the presence of the LORD God among the trees of the garden. But the LORD God called to the man and said to him, "Where are you?" And he said, "I heard the sound of you in the garden, and I was afraid, because I was naked, and I hid myself." He said, "Who told you that you were naked? Have you eaten of the tree of which I commanded you not to eat?" The man said, "The woman whom you gave to be with me, she gave me fruit of the tree, and I ate." Then the LORD God said to the woman, "What is this that you have done?" The woman said, "The serpent deceived me, and I ate."

—GENESIS 3:8–13

Notice the blame game that was started that day. God questioned Adam about how he knew that he was naked. Adam told God that the woman He had given him had caused him to sin. Implied here was that it was God's fault that Adam sinned. If God had not created Eve, Adam would not have sinned! In order to justify himself, he questioned the best gift he had ever received, his wife.

Eve got in on the act as she blamed the serpent for deceiving her. In her mind, if God had not created the serpent, she would have been OK. This situation was really God's fault, according to Adam and Eve. In truth, it was their issue. They had not trusted God. They had believed that they knew best. They thought they could make their own decisions and that they were better gods of their own lives than God.

> Therefore the LORD God sent him out from the garden of Eden to work the ground from which he was taken.
>
> —GENESIS 3:23

God did not just smile and look away at man's disagreement with Him. Adam and Eve were cast out of His presence. They no longer were able to enjoy God because of their rebellion against His leadership. Their decision now spelled war with God. They had disobeyed and tried to become their own gods. As a result, death now became part of mankind's reality. Before their sin, death did not even exist.

Many of us have tried to be our own gods and run our own lives. In doing so, we have taken our lives in a direction that God never intended. We have become drug addicts as we attempt to find the pleasures of life that God wanted to give us. We have reduced our marriages to a fight for power and recognition. We battle for possessions when God wants to give us everything we need. Just as Adam and Eve deviated from God's will, so do we.

Scripture goes on later to lay out the problem bluntly. There is not much room left for the person who thinks he can become godlike on his own.

> "None is righteous, no, not one;
>> no one understands;
>> no one seeks for God.
> All have turned aside; together they
>> have become worthless;
>> no one does good,
>> not even one."
> "Their throat is an open grave;
>> they use their tongues to
>> deceive."
> "The venom of asps is under their
>> lips."
>> "Their mouth is full of curses
>> and bitterness."
> "Their feet are swift to shed blood;
>> in their paths are ruin and
>> misery,

> and the way of peace they have not
> known."
> "There is no fear of God before
> their eyes."

—ROMANS 3:10–18

For all have sinned and fall short of the glory of God.

—ROMANS 3:23

The Bible says that *no one* (hear that?) has observed God's laws perfectly and *no one* really seeks after God. All the things that we do—attending church, trying not to lie or cuss, being good neighbors, helping little old ladies across the street—will not make us more like God. We cannot do enough to be perfect before God. Scripture also says in Romans 3:23 that we have fallen short or missed the mark of God's glory. Left to our own devices, we are not capable of knowing God. Our rebellion keeps us from Him. It separates us from Him.

That sounds like we are doomed to be enemies of God. The passage from Romans above tells us that without the direct intervention of God, we are stuck with a problem we cannot solve. In and of ourselves, we cannot repair our relationship with God any more than Adam and Eve could. We *must* have the help of God in order to be right with Him. We cannot do it ourselves.

A famous actor once mused that when he got to heaven, God would probably look at him, cross His arms, and frown. Then just as this actor believed that he was about to be sent to hell, God would say, "Ah, come on in, you knucklehead."

That will not happen to that actor nor to any of us. Something will have to change. We have declared war on God as a result of our sinful nature and through our actions. That declaration is eternal.

We need a way out.

CHAPTER 8

The Sacrifice for Sin

You are probably familiar with the term *scape-goat*. This is a word that describes someone who is blamed for something he did not do. I become my boys' scapegoat when we buy ice cream at the store. Back at home, Ryan and Chris accuse me in front of my wife, Suzie, of making the purchase. I get the blame, but I really had nothing to do with it. I'm innocent, I tell you ...

The origin of a scapegoat is actually biblical. In the book of Leviticus, the process of transferring the sins of the people is described. Once a year, on the Day of Atonement, the offenses of the people against God were put onto a goat that was then released into the desert.

The priest brought the scapegoat forward. He laid his hands on it and confessed the sins of the people, transferring their sins to it. The goat was then released into the desert. The procedure is described below:

"And when he has made an end of atoning for the Holy Place and the tent of meeting and the altar, he shall present the live goat. And Aaron shall lay both his hands on the head of the live goat, and confess over it all the iniquities of the people of Israel, and all their transgressions, all their sins. And he shall put them on the head of the goat and send it away into the wilderness by the hand of a man who is in readiness. The goat shall bear all their iniquities on itself to a remote area, and he shall let the goat go free in the wilderness."

—LEVITICUS 16:20–22

The Old Testament is full of references to sacrifices. Animals were brought before God and the sin of the person offering the sacrifice was placed upon the animal. The person's sin separated him from God, as was described in our previous chapter. In order to maintain a relationship with His people, God prescribed a system of atonement. Once their sacrifices were offered, they were forgiven of their sins and rebellion against God. This was a continual process. The annual scapegoat and other periodic sacrifices did not constitute a lasting solution to the problem of separation from God. Their sin continued; therefore their need for further forgiveness was perpetual.

The Old Testament had predicted that a Messiah would come who would free the people. As we have discussed, almost everyone believed that this would be a political freedom and that the Messiah would free Israel from the Romans. They missed the point. In Isaiah 53:4–6, written hundreds of years before Jesus arrived on earth, the Bible describes a Messiah who would be "crushed for our inequities" and "by [whose] wounds we are healed." The life of this Messiah would free the people, but not from the Romans; Jesus would free God's people from their own sins.

When Jesus was taken to the cross, it was not an accident or a mistake. It was through the actions of men who sought to rid the world of Jesus, but who actually were used by God to orchestrate His strategy for His people. As we will see, the cross was God's eternal plan that would once and for all serve as the *eternal* sacrifice for His people. It was God's design to come to earth as a man and to die for the sins of those who desire to pursue Jesus. No mistake. No Plan B. Just God's sovereign will enacted for His followers.

In the passages below, I have attempted to summarize the events of the cross. I would highly recommend that readers go to John 18 and 19 to read the entire account of the arrest, trial, and crucifixion of Jesus. It is the heart of the Christian faith. The events of that weekend stand as our reminder of God's love and forgiveness.

Jesus was arrested in the middle of the night and led off to a mock trial by the Jewish officials. They desired to have Jesus put to death since He was infringing on their ability to control the people. Jesus was taken to several judges, including Caiaphas, who was the high priest. Caiaphas, knowing that he could not sentence Jesus to death, sought the help of the Roman governor, Pilate:

> Then they led Jesus from the house of Caiaphas to the governor's headquarters. It was early morning. They themselves did not enter the governor's headquarters, so that they would not be defiled, but could eat the Passover. So Pilate went outside to them and said, "What accusation do you bring against this man?" They answered him, "If this man were not doing evil, we would not have delivered him over to you." Pilate said

to them, "Take him yourselves and judge him by your own law." The Jews said to him, "It is not lawful for us to put anyone to death." This was to fulfill the word that Jesus had spoken to show by what kind of death he was going to die.

So Pilate entered his headquarters again and called Jesus and said to him, "Are you the King of the Jews?" Jesus answered, "Do you say this of your own accord, or did others say it to you about me?" Pilate answered, "Am I a Jew? Your own nation and the chief priests have delivered you over to me. What have you done?" Jesus answered, "My kingdom is not of this world. If my kingdom were of this world, my servants would have been fighting, that I might not be delivered over to the Jews. But my kingdom is not from the world." Then Pilate said to him, "So you are a king?" Jesus answered, "You say that I am a king. For this purpose I was born and for this purpose I have come into the world—to bear witness to the truth. Everyone who is of the truth listens to my voice." Pilate said to him, "What is truth?"

—JOHN 18:28–38A

It is obvious from the above passage that Pilate believed Jesus was innocent of any wrongdoing. A central truth of the Bible is that Jesus was, in fact, not guilty. Jesus was to become the blameless sacrifice upon which the sins of God's people would be placed. The Bible says that Jesus never sinned; that He was "the righteous" being sacrificed for the "unrighteous" (1 Peter 3:18), to bring us to God. Jesus *was* innocent, but we are not. We need the Perfect Sacrifice to restore us to God.

In an attempt to appease them, Pilate gave in to the pressure of his rebellious subjects and had Jesus flogged. If Caesar in Rome heard that he was unable to control the Jews, he might lose his job or, worse, his life. But God used Pilate's need for self-preservation for a greater purpose.

> Then Pilate took Jesus and flogged him. And the soldiers twisted together a crown of thorns and put it on his head and arrayed him in a purple robe. They came up to him, saying, "Hail, King of the Jews!" and struck him with their hands. Pilate went out again and said to them, "See, I am bringing him out to you that you may know that I find

no guilt in him." So Jesus came out, wearing the crown of thorns and the purple robe. Pilate said to them, "Behold the man!" When the chief priests and the officers saw him, they cried out, "Crucify him, crucify him!" Pilate said to them, "Take him yourselves and crucify him, for I find no guilt in him." The Jews answered him, "We have a law, and according to that law he ought to die because he has made himself the Son of God." When Pilate heard this statement, he was even more afraid. He entered his headquarters again and said to Jesus, "Where are you from?" But Jesus gave him no answer. So Pilate said to him, "You will not speak to me? Do you not know that I have authority to release you and authority to crucify you?" Jesus answered him, "You would have no authority over me at all unless it had been given you from above."

—JOHN 19:1–11A

Pilate's attempt to save Jesus failed. He then allowed Jesus to be crucified. Jesus, the perfect Man—God on earth—was then placed on a wooden cross and was brutally killed. The punishment of death that each of us deserves, in our rebellion against God, was given to Jesus.

The sins that separate us from God were placed on Him by God to purchase for us an eternal freedom.

> So he delivered him over to them to be crucified. So they took Jesus, and he went out, bearing his own cross, to the place called The Place of a Skull, which in Aramaic is called Golgotha. There they crucified him, and with him two others, one on either side, and Jesus between them.
>
> —JOHN 19:16–18

After this, Jesus, knowing that all was now finished, said (to fulfill the Scripture), "I thirst." A jar full of sour wine stood there, so they put a sponge full of the sour wine on a hyssop branch and held it to his mouth. When Jesus had received the sour wine, he said, "It is finished," and he bowed his head and gave up his spirit.

Since it was the day of Preparation, and so that the bodies would not remain on the cross on the Sabbath (for that Sabbath was a high day), the Jews asked Pilate that their legs might be broken and that they might be taken away. So the soldiers came and broke the legs of the first, and of the other who had been crucified with him. But when they came to Jesus and saw that he was already dead, they did not break his legs. But one of the soldiers pierced his side with a spear, and at once there came out blood and water.

—JOHN 19:28–34

In verse 30 of John 19, Jesus said, "It is finished." The word in the Greek language was *tetelestai*. It was an accounting term meaning "paid in full." Jesus, on the cross, announced that His job was done and that He had paid our debt of sin in full. His death was the payment for our rebellion that separates us from God.

The apostle who was closest to Jesus throughout His life, Peter, witnessed the arrest and crucifixion. Peter summarized the death of Jesus in the following way:

He himself bore our sins in his body on the tree, that we might die to sin and live to righteousness. By his wounds you have been healed. For you were straying like sheep, but have now returned to the Shepherd and Overseer of your souls.

—1 PETER 2:24–25

The apostle Paul said it like this:

For while we were still weak, at the right time Christ died for the ungodly. For one will scarcely die for a righteous person—though perhaps for a good person one would dare even to die—but God shows his love for us in that while we were still sinners, Christ died for us.

—ROMANS 5:6–8

While we were still sinners, Christ died for us. Jesus came to die; to take our sins away so that we might live with Him ... forever. It was *our* sins that He bore on the cross. Jesus lived a perfect, sinless life, yet died the death of a common criminal. If you ever feel like no one cares, simply look at the cross. It is God's love letter to each of us who desires to embrace a relationship with Jesus. By His wounds, you have been healed.

The way is open for you to follow Jesus. The invitation offered to the fishermen on the shore of the lake is now extended to you, and, because of the cross, you can accept.

CHAPTER 9

Eyewitnesses

Eyewitnesses are key to every news story. We want to hear people who were there relate their opinions as to what happened and why. When friends of ours attend sporting events, we tend to ask them what it was like at the game. Even if we watched on television, we pose questions like, "What did it feel like when the winning score occurred?" or "What did the people around you say when that interception happened?" or "What was it like to actually be there?"

The crucifixion of Jesus was undoubtedly the most important event in history. Those who were there experienced a lasting life change. Their eyewitness reactions can give us great insight. In our last chapter, we read the biblical account of the cross. Now we will look at this incident again, this time through the eyes of those who were closest and had the best view.

Our first eyewitness was none other than the judge and jury himself, Pilate the governor. He had the unenviable position of trying to control a large crowd that wanted him to act outside of the law. He wanted to appease the crowd that had been swayed by the opinions of the priests and teachers.

> And he answered them, saying, "Do you want me to release for you the King of the Jews?" For he perceived that it was out of envy that the chief priests had delivered him up. But the chief priests stirred up the crowd to have him release for them Barabbas instead. And Pilate again said to them, "Then what shall I do with the man you call the King of the Jews?" And they cried out again, "Crucify him." And Pilate said to them, "Why, what evil has he done?" But they shouted all the more, "Crucify him." So Pilate, wishing to satisfy the crowd, released for them Barabbas, and having scourged Jesus, he delivered him to be crucified.
>
> —MARK 15:9–15

When he said, "What shall I do with the man you call the King of the Jews?" Pilate spoke for all of us. What are we going to do with this crucified man of history? We have a decision to make. Pilate wanted to release Him, but he was more afraid of public opinion than he was interested in doing the right thing.

Pilate is like those people who get swayed by the opinions of the crowd. Turn on television and someone tells you that you must be crazy to believe that God became a man and dwelt on earth. How ridiculous to believe that one man can take on the sins of the world! Our "friends" tell us to live it up because there is nothing but this life and when we die, we die. Others object that the Christian faith is intolerant of other faiths. There must be many ways to know God. And so we just agree in order to get along. We become like Pilate who allowed his decision to be dictated by a crowd that wanted to be in control. But we are still left with answering Pilate's question: What we are to do about Jesus?

Another set of eyewitnesses were the guards who actually prepared Jesus for the cross. These soldiers were stationed in Jerusalem on behalf of Rome. According to experts of history, Jerusalem was one of the worst assignments a Roman soldier could get. The people were rebellious and the climate was hot and dry. The Romans were sick of the Jews, who constantly complained and made their life difficult. When Jesus came along, the men in the execution detail took all their frustrations out on Him.

And the soldiers led him away inside the palace (that is, the governor's headquarters), and they called together the whole battalion. And they clothed him in a purple cloak, and twisting together a crown of thorns, they put it on him. And they began to salute him, "Hail, King of the Jews!" And they were striking his head with a reed and spitting on him and kneeling down in homage to him. And when they had mocked him, they stripped him of the purple cloak and put his own clothes on him. And they led him out to crucify him.

—MARK 15:16–20

Many people have difficult lives, made hard with the loss of jobs, deaths of loved ones, divorces, or years of addiction. How could a good God allow that? They ask, "If God is love, how could He allow all that goes on in this world?" These soldiers represent those people who are sick of a life that doesn't seem to make sense; therefore they lash out at those who hold up Jesus as a hope. Their anger comes flowing out whenever someone even mentions Jesus. This anger keeps them away from God. They miss the love of God due to their own misunderstanding.

There are others who feel like they are doing just fine without Jesus. When His story is thrust upon them, they are irritated because they have to deal with it. A witness to the crucifixion that day was also interrupted. His name was Simon and he was from the North African city of Cyrene (in modern-day Libya). He was brought closer than he ever wanted:

> And they compelled a passerby, Simon of Cyrene, who was coming in from the country, the father of Alexander and Rufus, to carry his cross.
>
> —MARK 15:21

This man Simon was "coming in from the country" on his way to somewhere else. He may have poked his head through the crowd just as Jesus was led by on the way to the execution. Jesus had been beaten severely and could not continue to carry the wooden cross and therefore needed help. Simon had to deal with the soldiers' "invitation" to carry the load of Jesus. He was forced into action. He could not overlook what was happening since he was now involved.

Those who are interrupted by the cross may tell us that faith in Jesus is fine for us, but they don't need it nor do they desire to hear about it. They want to be left alone and go their own way. But the cross *did* happen and we all *do* have to deal with it. No one can just put their hands over their ears and play like it did not happen. Even an attempt to ignore it constitutes a decision. It is a "no."

Some people, when presented with the life and death of Jesus, just don't care. They are like the soldiers who carried out the actual crucifixion. Listen to their account:

> And they brought him to the place called Golgotha (which means Place of a Skull). And they offered him wine mixed with myrrh, but he did not take it. And they crucified him and divided his garments among them, casting lots for them, to decide what each should take. And it was the third hour when they crucified him. And the inscription of the charge against him read, "The King of the Jews."
>
> —MARK 15:22–26

The Creator of the world was being crucified in front of them and they played dice for a chance to own His clothing. They had crucified many others before Jesus. He was just another face. No big deal.

Many in this world think that a relationship with Jesus is just another religion; just a way to deal with life. They are so preoccupied with life, jobs, and possessions that Jesus just seems like another theory. They quickly write Him off as a waste of time and go about their business. Yet Jesus cannot just be ignored. *If the story is true, it affects all of us.*

Sometimes people want to see something more from Jesus. They say, "If He would just come down here and speak to me, I might believe." The events of Jesus' life are just not enough for them. At the cross that day, there were some who mocked Jesus. They asked why didn't He come down and save Himself. They would have believed if He had come down (or so they said).

And those who passed by derided him, wagging their heads and saying, "Aha! You who would destroy the temple and rebuild it in three days, save yourself, and come down from the cross!" So also the chief priests with the scribes mocked him to one another, saying, "He saved others; he cannot save himself. Let the Christ, the King of Israel, come down now from the cross that we may see and believe."

—MARK 15:29–32A

Interestingly enough, I think those mentioned above really wanted Jesus to free Himself. They could trust a Savior that performed miracles (as they prescribed them). They called on Jesus to come down and save Himself. Maybe they figured such an act would save them too.

Many people are just not able to accept Jesus as He is. They want to be able to tell Him what He should do and how He should act. They have a preconceived idea of what God should do. But if God is the Creator, shouldn't *He* be the One who makes the rules? How can we, the created ones, tell the Creator how things should be? But we do ... and frequently.

Finally, there were two who had the best view of this great event. Unfortunately for them, they were closer than they cared to be. They were the two thieves who were crucified with Jesus. They were able to observe Him firsthand. Look at their reactions:

> One of the criminals who were hanged railed at him, saying, "Are you not the Christ? Save yourself and us!" But the other rebuked him, saying, "Do you not fear God, since you are under the same sentence of condemnation? And we indeed justly, for we are receiving the due reward of our deeds; but this man has done nothing wrong." And he said,

"Jesus, remember me when you come into your kingdom." And he said to him, "Truly, I say to you, today you will be with me in Paradise."

—LUKE 23:39–43

One of the thieves joined in the mockery. Maybe it gave him some comfort in being a part of the crowd. But by the day's end, the priests would go home and the thief would be face to face with God.

The other thief reacted differently. After witnessing Jesus' actions all day, he concluded that Jesus was who He said He was. At the last moment of his life, he turned to Jesus and asked to be with Him. He wanted to go to the kingdom of God with Jesus. He was graciously granted that desire. Jesus assured him that on that very day he would see Paradise. For those who want to give up on all their failures and struggles, Jesus stands ready to grant them a personal relationship with Him.

Some of Jesus' last words were, "My God, my God, why have You forsaken Me?" (Mark 15:34). At that moment, Jesus endured the sins of the world and was separated from His Father. His cry, "Why have You forsaken Me?" assures us that we will never have to ask that question ourselves. Read that statement again. His death opens a way for us to never be forsaken by our Eternal Father. Jesus endured the separation that we deserve. The Scriptures say that when Jesus died, the temple curtain, which covered the Holy of Holies, was ripped in half, from top to bottom (Mark 15:38). A curtain, which was approximately a foot thick, was miraculously opened up. The Holy of Holies was the sacred room in the temple in which God's Presence dwelt. The torn curtain signaled that God had opened His heart to us and each believer no longer had to be represented by a priest. The way to God was opened for the followers of Jesus.

> And Jesus uttered a loud cry and breathed his last. And the curtain of the temple was torn in two, from top to bottom. And when the centurion, who stood facing him, saw that in this way he breathed his last, he said, "Truly this man was the Son of God!"
>
> —MARK 15:37–39

One of the last and most significant comments made that day came from one of the Roman soldiers, a centurion. He must have stood near the cross all day and observed Jesus. After seeing Jesus in His dying moment, this centurion came to the conclusion that he had just witnessed the death of the Son of God. He had watched. He had listened. And he was convinced.

Where are you in this cast of characters? Are you irritated with Jesus for interrupting your life? Maybe you just don't care and are reading this account to appease the person who gave it to you. Are the worries of the world obstructing your view of Jesus?

Or are you beginning to listen to the reality that maybe Jesus is indeed inviting you to a great decision point of your life?

The final chapter in Jesus' life had not yet been seen. We have one more great event to observe.

CHAPTER 10

The Loophole

A legendary story concerning W.C. Fields has been passed around for many years. One day, one of the famous comedian's friends found him diligently pouring over a Bible. The friend, knowing that Fields was not very interested in spiritual things, was shocked. He asked him why he was reading the Bible. Fields responded, "Loopholes ... looking for loopholes ..."

Those who hear the story of the gospel should know that they are left with only two choices. One is to accept Jesus Christ as who He said He was and follow Him. The other is to ignore the life of Jesus and to reject the claims of the Bible. Those are the only two choices. There is no middle ground.

Jesus cannot be just a good teacher who spoke inspirationally. He said He was God. A good teacher doesn't say things like that. If you had a professor who claimed that he was God, you would *not* think he was a good teacher. You would think that he was deluded. To say that Jesus taught good things but that He was not God is simply intellectual suicide. He either is or He isn't.

Many are seeking a loophole; some sort of way to reject Jesus once and for all so that His claims on their life can be disregarded. All right, here is that loophole: If you can disprove the resurrection of Jesus, you do not have to believe in His claim of deity. If Jesus did not rise from the dead, you don't have to follow Him, since you'd be pursuing a dead Savior. Jesus is either living, in which case we must follow Him, or He is dead and therefore has no relevance in our lives.

The problem is that most people have never looked seriously at the accounts of the resurrection of Jesus. This is dangerous business for the person who thinks one can just remain neutral on the subject. For if one *does* inspect the record of the claim that Jesus returned from the dead, the person must now make a decision! The only way to make an informed decision would be to actually know the story. I propose that we spend a few pages here in order to examine the details.

Here is the way the Gospel of Matthew presents the burial of Jesus:

When it was evening, there came a rich man from Arimathea, named Joseph, who also was a disciple of Jesus. He went to Pilate and asked for the body of Jesus. Then Pilate ordered it to be given to him. And Joseph took the body and wrapped it in a clean linen shroud and laid it in his own new tomb, which he had cut in the rock. And he rolled a great stone to the entrance of the tomb and went away. Mary Magdalene and the other Mary were there, sitting opposite the tomb.

The next day, that is, after the day of Preparation, the chief priests and the Pharisees gathered before Pilate and said, "Sir, we remember how that impostor said, while he was still alive, 'After three days I will rise.' Therefore order the tomb to be made secure until the third day, lest his disciples go and steal him away and tell the people, 'He has risen from the dead,' and the last fraud will be worse than the first." Pilate said to them, "You have a guard of soldiers. Go, make it as secure as you can." So they went and made the tomb secure by sealing the stone and setting a guard.

—MATTHEW 27:57–66

After His death was confirmed by the Roman soldiers, the body of Jesus was removed from the cross and placed in a tomb belonging to one of His followers, Joseph from Arimathea. Since it was about to be the Sabbath, Jesus' body was quickly taken down and placed in a rock tomb with plans to complete the proper burial after the Sabbath. The Jewish people could not work on the Sabbath. Handling a dead body would not only constitute work, it would make them "unclean" for the Sabbath. Pilate gave his permission for the body to be given to Joseph and it was placed in a sealed tomb. There were several women who witnessed this procedure.

There had been talk about Jesus rising from the dead, so the priests and Pharisees were concerned that the body might be stolen. They asked for a detail of soldiers to be placed at the tomb and this was done. So from the time that Jesus was laid in this sealed tomb, there were guards at the entrance making sure that no one tampered with the body. This was to become a crucial issue.

Let's continue with our look at Matthew's account of the Resurrection story:

Now after the Sabbath, toward the dawn of the first day of the week, Mary Magdalene and the other Mary went to see the tomb. And behold, there was a great earthquake, for an angel of the Lord descended from heaven and came and rolled back the stone and sat on it. His appearance was like lightning, and his clothing white as snow. And for fear of him the guards trembled and became like dead men. But the angel said to the women, "Do not be afraid, for I know that you seek Jesus who was crucified. He is not here, for he has risen, as he said. Come, see the place where he lay. Then go quickly and tell his disciples that he has risen from the dead, and behold, he is going before you to Galilee; there you will see him. See, I have told you." So they departed quickly from the tomb with fear and great joy, and ran to tell his disciples. And behold, Jesus met them and said, "Greetings!" And they came up and took hold of his feet and worshiped him. Then Jesus said to them, "Do not be afraid; go and tell my brothers to go to Galilee, and there they will see me."

While they were going, behold, some of the guard went into the city and told the chief priests all that had taken place. And when they had assembled with the elders and taken counsel, they gave a sufficient sum of money to the soldiers and said, "Tell people, 'His disciples came by night and stole him away while we were asleep.' And if this comes to the governor's ears, we will satisfy him and keep you out of trouble." So they took the money and did as they were directed. And this story has been spread among the Jews to this day.

—MATTHEW 28:1–15

So what happened? It is a simple story. Jesus was laid in the tomb on Friday night and then, on Sunday morning, some women came to the grave to anoint the body. When they arrived the stone that sealed the tomb had been moved. The guards that had been in front of the tomb were at a loss as to what to say. Fearfully, they went to the priests and told them what had taken place. At the same time, the women met Jesus and talked to Him and touched Him. The apostle Paul, in 1 Corinthians 15:5–6, says that Jesus appeared to His apostles and then to over five hundred people. This is a sizable amount of witnesses. There have been many major historical events that have been reported by far fewer people.

So again, what happened? Aside from the fact that the Bible is one of the most authenticated documents in history and it details the story, how can the events be explained? Below are several theories doubters have suggested to explain away the Resurrection. As you read them, you will see that they are all easily refuted and understand why the friends of Jesus believed that He had indeed risen from the dead and why His enemies were sent scrambling for an explanation of the event.

First, some have suggested that the women simply arrived at *the wrong tomb*. They just made a mistake. It could happen to anyone. They were distraught on Friday night and they got mixed up about the location of the tomb.

The wrong-tomb theory has several problems. Notice that it wasn't just the women who reported Jesus gone; the guards also thought the body was missing! And what about the testimony of more than five hundred people who said they saw Jesus? Finally, a mistaken location would have been easy to remedy. The authorities could have just produced the body from the right tomb and the whole thing would have been over.

Another theory to explain away the Resurrection is to declare that the five hundred experienced a *mass hallucination* and only *thought* they saw Jesus. The women suggested it, and all of those people constructed it in their minds. This idea, too, has logical problems. Wouldn't the authorities just produce a body? Why would the priests and Pharisees who engineered the crucifixion allow such a tale to continue? They would not, and certainly the Romans would not want that, either. And by the way, when has such a hallucination ever occurred? By five hundred people?

A third idea: *Jesus never died; He just swooned or passed out.* The crucifixion caused Him to appear dead, but He really wasn't. Those Roman guards made a mistake and thought Jesus was dead. Then, in the cool of the tomb, He was revived. He then rolled away the stone blocking the tomb's entrance and He presented Himself to the women, the five hundred, and others as a risen Savior.

Answering this objection is easy. These soldiers knew death. When they came to Jesus on the cross, they declared Him dead and then pierced His side with a spear just to make sure (John 19:33–34). Further, think of the condition Jesus would have been in, had He actually survived. He had been brutally beaten within an inch of His life, had carried a heavy cross until He dropped, had been nailed to it, and had hung there for over six hours. He would not have had food or water since His last supper with the apostles on Thursday night.

How could a man in this condition then have the ability to somehow move the heavy stone— and from the inside, in the dark? He would then have had to elude the guards and get away, all in a weakened state that mere hours before convinced everyone He was dead. Though He had barely lived through the crucifixion experience, He appeared to be vibrant, and everyone who saw Him believed that He had risen from the dead. Some people believe this explanation, but it is highly unlikely. OK, totally unlikely.

Here's the final theory. *The disciples stole the body.* The disciples wanted to continue Jesus' ministry and they knew that if people saw that He was dead, they would no longer believe in Him. Sometime between Friday night and Sunday morning, they came and took the body and hid it. They overpowered the guards. They had someone masquerading to be Jesus appear to the women and all the other witnesses. And folks who had known Jesus for many years believed that they had seen Him.

Wait a minute. The apostles *ran* when Jesus was arrested. Only two had the courage to follow Jesus to the courtyard where He was on trial. Peter, one of the two, wouldn't even admit to a slave girl that he knew Jesus, as we will see in the next chapter. These were the men who supposedly came back together and plotted to steal the body? These were the guys who didn't even understand that Jesus would die (Luke 18:31–34)? When would they have made this plan? Where did they get the courage to carry it out? Is this a feasible story? It is not.

You might want to say that you do not even believe these events occurred. Jesus was not a real person who was truly crucified. It just did not happen. Yet the history books detail the life of a man named Jesus. You can look into the secular record and find accounts of this crucifixion. His death and burial are facts. It is the Resurrection that is in question.

So if anyone could come up with a loophole theory to not believe that Jesus came back from the dead, why haven't they? Because *there is no loophole!* No one has been able to disprove the Resurrection. Surely by now, if Jesus had not risen, the real truth would have come out.

Here's the good news. The truth *has* come out: Jesus rose from the dead. He died for our sins. It was God's plan that was carried out by the priests and Pharisees, even when they didn't know it. Take a look at the complete summary by Paul in 1 Corinthians:

Now I would remind you, brothers, of the gospel I preached to you, which you received, in which you stand, and by which you are being saved, if you hold fast to the word I preached to you—unless you believed in vain.

For I delivered to you as of first importance what I also received: that Christ died for our sins in accordance with the Scriptures, that he was buried, that he was raised on the third day in accordance with the Scriptures, and that he appeared to Cephas, then to the twelve. Then he appeared to more than five hundred brothers at one time, most of whom are still alive, though some have fallen asleep. Then he appeared to James, then to all the apostles. Last of all, as to one untimely born, he appeared also to me. For I am the least of the apostles, unworthy to be called an apostle, because I persecuted the church of God. But by the grace of God I am what I am, and his grace toward me was not in vain. On the contrary, I worked harder than any of them, though it was not I, but the grace of God that is with me. Whether then it was I or they, so we preach and so you believed.

—1 CORINTHIANS 15:1–11

Paul's account was written just a few years after Jesus was on earth. Those around him believed the Resurrection to be true. They knew there was no loophole. We, too must come to grips with what happened on that weekend long ago.

Your invitation is almost in place. We need only to make one more stop.

CHAPTER 11

Scared Men Changing the World

One of the most compelling reasons to believe that Jesus really did rise from the dead is found in the lives of the apostles who followed Him around for three years. What happened to those fishermen when Jesus was taken before the chief priests and Pilate? Where were they the day that Jesus hung on the cross?

Just to remind ourselves of the state of the apostles on the night Jesus was arrested, let's take another quick look. The Bible says that as Jesus was taken away, they all left Him and fled (Matthew 26:56). There was even an unnamed young man who ran away, leaving his clothing behind:

> And a young man followed him, with nothing but a linen cloth about his body. And

they seized him, but he left the linen cloth
and ran away naked.

—MARK 14:51

Peter, who was one of those original fishermen we met in our first chapter, actually was
frightened by a young servant girl. Take a look
at his story:

And as Peter was below in the courtyard,
one of the servant girls of the high priest
came, and seeing Peter warming himself,
she looked at him and said, "You also were
with the Nazarene, Jesus." But he denied
it, saying, "I neither know nor understand
what you mean." And he went out into the
gateway and the rooster crowed. And the
servant girl saw him and began again to
say to the bystanders, "This man is one of
them." But again he denied it. And after
a little while the bystanders again said to
Peter, "Certainly you are one of them, for
you are a Galilean." But he began to invoke
a curse on himself and to swear, "I do not
know this man of whom you speak." And
immediately the rooster crowed a second
time. And Peter remembered how Jesus had

said to him, "Before the rooster crows twice,
you will deny me three times." And he broke
down and wept.

—MARK 14:66–72

So much for bravery. They all ran away. One
ran naked because they grabbed his garment. Peter
completely denied that he even knew Jesus. With
cursing, he violently objected that he had ever followed Jesus. These are not courageous acts.

So what became of these men who all ran
away?

Believe it or not, within a few months of
these events, these men became world changers.
How could these men have ever gotten brave
enough to resume following Jesus?

Peter, who famously denied Christ three
times on the night of His betrayal, is seen a
short while later giving a sermon after which
over three thousand people decided to join the
disciples in following Jesus! Peter concluded his
message to the huge crowd with these words:

"Let all the house of Israel therefore know
for certain that God has made him both Lord
and Christ, this Jesus whom you crucified."

—ACTS 2:36

And look what happened:

> Now when they heard this they were cut to the heart, and said to Peter and the rest of the apostles, "Brothers, what shall we do?" And Peter said to them, "Repent and be baptized every one of you in the name of Jesus Christ for the forgiveness of your sins, and you will receive the gift of the Holy Spirit. For the promise is for you and for your children and for all who are far off, everyone whom the Lord our God calls to himself." And with many other words he bore witness and continued to exhort them, saying, "Save yourselves from this crooked generation." So those who received his word were baptized, and there were added that day about three thousand souls.
>
> —ACTS 2:37–41

The story isn't done. Peter and John, on their way to the temple, encountered a crippled man:

> Now Peter and John were going up to the temple at the hour of prayer, the ninth hour. And a man lame from birth was being carried, whom they laid daily at the gate of the temple that is called the Beautiful Gate to

ask alms of those entering the temple. Seeing Peter and John about to go into the temple, he asked to receive alms. And Peter directed his gaze at him, as did John, and said, "Look at us." And he fixed his attention on them, expecting to receive something from them. But Peter said, "I have no silver and gold, but what I do have I give to you. In the name of Jesus Christ of Nazareth, rise up and walk!" And he took him by the right hand and raised him up, and immediately his feet and ankles were made strong. And leaping up he stood and began to walk, and entered the temple with them, walking and leaping and praising God. And all the people saw him walking and praising God, and recognized him as the one who sat at the Beautiful Gate of the temple, asking for alms. And they were filled with wonder and amazement at what had happened to him.

—ACTS 3:1–10

What kind of power is this? How could these simple and frightened men have been transformed into men who converted thousands? And if these guys could change, maybe it says something about us. I mean, we are pretty scared from time to time. Maybe we won't have enough courage to take on this adventure with Jesus. What if it causes us to have to give a speech in front of three thousand people?

Two events happened to give these simple men courage. First, they witnessed and interacted with the resurrected Jesus. They saw Him firsthand and knew it was Him. They had been told by the women that Jesus was alive. Peter and John had seen Him as well. The disciples met and were trying to figure out what do to:

> As they were talking about these things, Jesus himself stood among them, and said to them, "Peace to you!" But they were startled and frightened and thought they saw a spirit. And he said to them, "Why are you troubled, and why do doubts arise in your hearts? See my hands and my feet, that it is I myself. Touch me, and see. For a spirit does not have flesh and bones as you see that I have." And when he had said this, he showed them his hands and his feet. And while they still disbelieved for joy and were marveling, he said to them, "Have you anything here to eat?" They gave him a piece of broiled fish, and he took it and ate before them.
>
> Then he said to them, "These are my words that I spoke to you while I was still with you, that everything written about

me in the Law of Moses and the Prophets and the Psalms must be fulfilled." Then he opened their minds to understand the Scriptures, and said to them, "Thus it is written, that the Christ should suffer and on the third day rise from the dead, and that repentance and forgiveness of sins should be proclaimed in his name to all nations, beginning from Jerusalem. You are witnesses of these things. And behold, I am sending the promise of my Father upon you. But stay in the city until you are clothed with power from on high."

—LUKE 24:36–49

These men witnessed Jesus as truly risen. He had a body. He was not a hallucination. They watched Him eat. They touched Him. They were not making up a story. They were not even looking for this—He totally startled them. This was the last thing they expected. But here, right in their midst, Jesus stood. No one had seen Him walk in the door. He just appeared.

Jesus helped them to understand all the Old Testament prophecies, which had predicted His coming. The Bible says that Jesus "opened their minds to understand." Not only did they see Jesus, but they understood because He gave them understanding!

Then He called them to a mission. He told them that they would tell His story, but this would happen only after power came from "on high." Who knew what that meant? They continued to see Him on some other occasions and finally witnessed Him being taken up into the sky (Acts 1). Now they were alone. Jesus wasn't with them. Surely now the dream would die. In fact, it had only begun!

> When the day of Pentecost arrived, they were all together in one place. And suddenly there came from heaven a sound like a mighty rushing wind, and it filled the entire house where they were sitting. And divided tongues as of fire appeared to them and rested on each one of them. And they were all filled with the Holy Spirit and began to speak in other tongues as the Spirit gave them utterance.
>
> —ACTS 2:1–4

The second experience that gave them new courage was that the very Presence of God came upon these men. They were literally possessed—not by some strange demons, but by God Himself! They became men who were transformed by the Spirit of God. They started to speak in foreign languages (that they didn't know). Now they could communicate with the rest of the world. They were miraculously changed.

How did they do the miracles and give the life-changing sermons? God did it through them. As they committed their lives to following Jesus, they were transformed and began doing what, until that point, only Jesus had done. They were actually becoming like Jesus! They were still imperfect, but by the power of God, their lives were changed so that they could begin to build God's kingdom. Their impact upon the world was greater than they could have ever imagined. They were set on fire spiritually by God in order to become what He had always planned for them to be. Here's how Paul said it:

> Therefore, if anyone is in Christ, he is a new creation. The old has passed away; behold, the new has come.
>
> —2 CORINTHIANS 5:17

Could we ever become what they became? Are we to be used like they were? The answer is a resounding yes! God is still in the business of transformation. Your life can truly count for something great. The old can be gone and a new life can begin to happen. You can be an ambassador for God. You can actually represent Him to a depraved world that is crying out for help.

What if you are invited to become a world changer?

CHAPTER 12

The Invitation Revisited

Remember where we started in this book? Jesus came to some fishermen and invited them to follow Him. They didn't know everything about Him. They were not graduates of a seminary. And they may not have even been nice people. Jesus just walked up to them and asked them if they would like to follow Him. Implied in this invitation was that they would obey His teaching and learn about His way of life.

While other rabbis were telling people that they were *not* good enough to follow them, Jesus said the opposite. These disciples *were* good enough to follow Him. They were made righteous by Jesus Himself. We all are qualified to follow Jesus because God says, *through Jesus*, we are forgiven and made to be worthy in God's eyes. No matter what the world says, you are good enough.

What did the disciples do to accept the invitation of Jesus? They just started to follow Him. He did not ask them to come up to the front of a church. Jesus didn't warn them, at that time, that they would go to hell if they didn't follow Him. He just offered an invitation and they accepted. They began to go along with Him ... everywhere He went ... and watched everything He did ... and their lives were rocked.

You have just been through a brief summary of what they witnessed. A full report of what they saw is found in the Gospel narratives of Matthew, Mark, Luke, and John. You can read those accounts in the Bible. Each details the life of Jesus, His miracles, His relationships, His teachings, and in the end, His crucifixion and His resurrection.

Today, you have an offer similar to the one Jesus made to those fishermen. Jesus may be calling to ask you to follow Him. Through His sacrifice on the cross He made it possible for you to have a lasting relationship with Him. Your sins can be forgiven. You can have a new start to your life. You can be reborn! The day that you begin following Jesus, your transformation will begin. It will be a process, but it will have a starting place.

So how do you take Jesus up on this invitation? What do you have to do? You might say,

"Do I have to fill out a card? Or pray a prayer? Or phone a friend?"

Here it is ... Here's how to do it ... Are you listening?

Ask God to forgive you for your rebellion and then begin to follow Jesus. Pray a prayer something like this:

"Jesus, I know I have sinned against You and I want to change. I believe that You are God come to earth, that You died for my sin, and rose from the dead. I want to follow You from this day forward. Amen."

Through His death and resurrection, He has opened up the way to God. Yes, you are imperfect and yes, you will continue to make mistakes and yes, sometimes, you will deliberately do what Jesus told you not to do. But Jesus will forgive you. God declares you forgiven because of Jesus' sacrifice and your belief. You can follow Jesus because He accepts you and offers you a new life.

A story from the Old Testament will illustrate the simplicity of accepting the forgiveness of God and beginning a great journey with Jesus. The Israelites had left Egypt with Moses and they had been in the desert a long time. On several occasions, they rebelled. During one difficult period, they openly berated Moses, asking him why he had brought them out of their slavery:

> From Mount Hor they set out by the way to
> the Red Sea, to go around the land of Edom.
> And the people became impatient on the
> way. And the people spoke against God and
> against Moses, "Why have you brought us
> up out of Egypt to die in the wilderness? For
> there is no food and no water, and we loathe
> this worthless food."
>
> —NUMBERS 21:4–5

The "worthless food" that they "loathed" was
the manna that God sent them every night. Their
complaints represented open rebellion. As they
grumbled to Moses, they were actually rebelling
against God and against the way He was taking
them. As punishment for this sin, God sent poi-
sonous snakes into their camp:

> Then the LORD sent venomous snakes
> among them; they bit the people and many
> Israelites died.
>
> —NUMBERS 21:6 (NIV 1984)

When the people realized what they had
done, they came to Moses and asked him to pray
to God for them:

> The people came to Moses and said, "We
> sinned when we spoke against the LORD and

against you. Pray that the LORD will take the snakes away from us." So Moses prayed for the people.

—NUMBERS 21:7 (NIV 1984)

God gave Moses a remedy for the people so they could live:

The LORD said to Moses, "Make a snake and put it up on a pole, anyone who is bitten can look at it and live." So Moses made a bronze snake and put it up on a pole. Then when anyone was bitten by a snake and looked at the bronze snake, he lived.

—NUMBERS 21:8–9 (NIV 1984)

So what did the people have to do? To obtain the healing grace of God, all they had to do was to *look up* at the serpent. When they did that, they were saved. The snake bites no longer had an effect on them. They had done a terrible thing. They had ridiculed the food that God had given them. They had loudly rebelled. God's way had been rejected. But a mere look at the serpent, God's saving provision, would cure them. They were forgiven and were given a new chance at life.

Here's a piece of good news for you: God, in His great love, sent His Son Jesus into the world to heal the relationship between God and those who looked toward Jesus. The healing of God is extended to us in Jesus. You can be forgiven and you can have a new life. God offers you a place in His kingdom. Ephesians 2 says:

> But God, being rich in mercy, because of the great love with which he loved us, even when we were dead in our trespasses, made us alive together with Christ—by grace you have been saved.
>
> —EPHESIANS 2:4–5

The Bible says that we were dead in our sins and rebellion against the Creator, who gave us life. God, in His great love for us, made us alive. Grace is described as God's unmerited favor. We did not do anything to earn it. We had nothing coming to us, but because of His perfect love, God extended us His friendship. Through Jesus, God allows us to follow Him and to learn from Him. Jesus will transform our lives. He will make us to be what God had originally intended. The Bible says that we are the masterpieces of God—His handiwork—designed to do good works. Take a look:

For by grace you have been saved through faith. And this is not your own doing; it is the gift of God, not a result of works, so that no one may boast. For we are his workmanship, created in Christ Jesus for good works, which God prepared beforehand, that we should walk in them.

—EPHESIANS 2:8–10

Your invitation has arrived.

Will you accept? Here's what the Bible says about accepting the invitation:

If you confess with your mouth that Jesus is Lord and believe in your heart that God raised him from the dead, you will be saved. For with the heart one believes and is justified, and with the mouth one confesses and is saved.

—ROMANS 10:9–10

We declare Him as the Lord of our life and begin to follow Him. We must believe that Jesus is the Son of God, raised from the dead to live as our Lord. We put our lives in His hands and are declared by God to be sinless (justified). This is a guaranteed contract of God. We are called to believe in the deity of Jesus and then to publicly affirm our allegiance to Him. God forgives us and allows us to walk with Jesus.

What a deal! To walk with the Creator of the Universe. That is the call of a lifetime.

CHAPTER 13

Invited to Know Life

What would happen if one day the governor of your state really *did* call you and invite you to join in on a great project? How would you react? And what might you be asked to do?

What if you were invited to help men and women in the inner cities of your state? With a budget that could really make a difference, you would be granted the authority of the governor to enact legislation and policies that could improve the lives of thousands. You might get to see homeless men and women cared for in a real and meaningful way.

Or what if you were to become the governor's spokesman for ramping up the economy of the state? Maybe you are asked to meet with business leaders from your area to seek their suggestions on how to make the commercial climate of your state more conducive to profitable businesses. As you work, you could see the economic environment altered in such a way that everyone who works and lives in that state could live better lives.

When faced with an invitation like we posed in the first chapter, it seems like there is no way that someone would refuse. But there is a "cost" to this decision. One's old life would be gone. Once you had experienced the excitement of working with the governor you could no longer go back to the mundane life you were living. Somehow, sitting on the sofa and watching a football game might no longer be satisfying.

Once you have risked losing your old routines in exchange for a life filled with new adventure, you probably would never want to undo that decision. Just the same, the risk was real. There was a leap that had to be taken. You had to release your grip on what seemed secure in order to grasp the future.

Think about trapeze artists in the circus. Their acts are sensational and death-defying. One performer swings out on a bar toward her partner on another bar. She releases her grip, flying high into the air and at just the right time, with split-second timing, her partner catches her, her old bar left empty, swinging back and forth.

Something happened right before she joined her partner. Did you see it? Don't miss it. The entertainer had to *let go* of the bar that she was on. At that moment, she was merely hanging in space. Life was a risk. Before those below could even understand the performer's dilemma, her partner came along on his bar and whisked her off, and all applauded. Only one person really understood the risk. Yep, you guessed it … the performer knows that a chance was taken.

But really, what was the alternative? To just sit on the first bar and safely swing and wave? Who would go to see that? The excitement and adventure is found in the unknown. The performer might have fallen! Had it not been for her expertise and willingness to take a risk, we would not be entertained. We are attracted because she is putting everything on the line, even her very life. Nobody pays for "safe." No one applauds security.

If life was meant to be lived, then shouldn't we want to go live it? We want to know the adventure of risking it all and coming out on top. We read books about it. We pay to see movies about it. Sporting events remind us that each of us has a longing to leave it all out there on the field in search of achievement and victory.

Yet most of us observe from the sofa.

What is holding you back from grabbing on to this call of a lifetime with Jesus Christ? Is it fear of failure? Probably not. After all, if Jesus rose from the dead, you can bet that nothing is too difficult for Him. He will not let us down like a governor might; He will not be late, like a trapeze artist's partner might be. We may experience momentary setbacks, but the sure promise of God is for eternal joy and satisfaction.

Do we believe that our commitment to a life with Jesus would be fruitless and boring? Ask the disciples how it worked out for them. Peter walked on water. Phillip, Andrew, and the rest of the apostles helped feed at least five thousand people one day with only five loaves and two fish (Mark 6). Lazarus was raised from the dead, and his sisters Martha and Mary saw their brother walk out of his grave (John 11). Boring? I don't think so!

Here's why we may turn down this invitation. We are desperately afraid of missing out on the comforts of life. If we follow Jesus, will we still get to go on a fancy vacation to Hawaii? I don't know. Will we get to own a personal jet? I still don't know. Will everyone like and respect us? I cannot make that promise. Will we get to retire and take it easy? Maybe not.

So what guarantees can I make to you about the Christian life?

I can make *only one*. I do not know how long you will live, how much savings you will have, if you will be famous or even be known outside your neighborhood. The one guarantee I can positively make is that you will have lived your life abundantly here on earth in relationship with the Lord of Life (John 10:10). And when it comes time to move out of this world—and that time *will* come—you will go to be with Him eternally. You will understand how each and every event of your earthly life has added up to a perfect eternity with the One who created you with a great purpose.

Each of us lives for jobs that won't satisfy. We trust friends who let us down. We buy possessions that will soon be gone. Yet when offered a true, lasting relationship with the Creator of the Universe, we say we can't give those things up.

I have heard that when trappers go to the jungle to catch monkeys, the process is simple (somebody let me know if this is true). Into a bottle with a small opening, a banana is placed. The monkey will reach in to grab the banana and by making a fist, becomes trapped by his own greed. His hand will not slip out of the jar as long as he holds the banana. The trapper returns, and the monkey is just standing there, clutching the banana. I like to imagine the monkeys looking down in embarrassment as they are led away, still holding the banana. A sad sight indeed.

I am not sure that we are much better off than the monkeys. We all want to live the best life that we can, so we grab all the possessions and power that we can hold. Unfortunately we wind up just standing there with our fist in the bottle, grasping those things that will never last but now hold us captive. While some people in the world are living life to its fullest, others are embarrassed for living a life that is full of misery, yet they cannot let go.

As we close this book, my challenge is for you to consider the life that has been described. Let go of the insignificant things that hold you back. Forget about momentary pleasure and grab onto an eternal relationship with the God who created you. In Him and Him alone will you find what you are looking for. By following Jesus, you will understand what life is all about and will know how you fit into this vast creation.

The apostle Paul wrote to his young protégé Timothy and addressed an issue that, almost two thousand years later, is still true.

> Command those who are rich in this present world not to be arrogant nor to put their hope in wealth, which is so uncertain, but to put their hope in God, who richly provides us with everything for our enjoyment.

Command them to do good, to be rich in
good deeds, and to be generous and willing
to share. In this way they will lay up treasure for themselves as a firm foundation for
the coming age, so that they may take hold
of the life that is truly life.

—1 TIMOTHY 6:17–19 (NIV 1984)

Each of us wants to know "the life that is
truly life." In the quest for it, some miss that life.
Some will hold the momentary and think that it
is eternal. Paul told it like it is. Don't trust the
temporary.

Put your hope in Jesus Christ. He will
empower you to change. Attempt to do the
things that Jesus would have you do. He will live
through you and will accomplish more than you
could ever dream. And as we live, each of us will
be laying up treasure in heaven. I do not know
exactly how that works, but I am sure that this
life is slowly going away. I am growing older. I
see people move on from this life every day. I do
not want to miss what God has in mind for me.

So I will follow Jesus, and through faith, will
build a foundation for a life that will never end
and never decay. I will let go of what seems so
certain, but in reality is just smoke and mirrors.
Just an empty bar swinging back and forth.

My desire for you is that you will lay your hopes and dreams on the Creator God who loves you and who calls out from eternity for you to follow His Son. We are offered a relationship with God who, though we were at war with Him, has ended our alienation from Him through the life, death, and resurrection of Jesus, the very presence of God on earth. We take up God's offer by believing on the Lord Jesus and asking Him for His grace to forgive us, and He will begin to live through us.

Now *that* is the life that is truly life! And to that life you are invited.

Discussion Questions

Chapter 1

Who is the most famous person that you have ever met? What are the details of the meeting?

If you could meet anyone on earth, living or dead, who would it be? Why?

What does the "man on the street" think about God and Christianity?

Why do people not investigate the Christian life?

Chapter 2

Have you ever been invited to a party or a meeting that you didn't feel qualified to attend? When?

If Jesus were in the world today, where do you think He would go, and what do you think He would do?

What risks did the fishermen take when they followed Jesus? Try to guess the conversation that they had with their father as they left him on the boat.

Why do you think the fishermen followed Jesus?

Chapter 3
If you were God, how would you have revealed yourself to the world?

What amazes you most about God becoming a man?

Who has stood by and supported you when others turned away?

Why was it so hard for the disciples who lived with Jesus to recognize Him as God?

Chapter 4

Why did the people in Israel not understand who Jesus was? (Hint: Was He the One they were expecting?)

What do your friends think about the kingdom of God? How would they describe it?

Do the actions of Jesus match the image that people have of Him? Why or why not?

What is surprising about the way Jesus behaved at the wedding party?

Chapter 5

Do you believe in a physical heaven and hell? What evidence do you have to support your opinion?

Why is the threat of punishment not a good motivator? How does your thinking apply to the spiritual life?

What do you think heaven will be like? What about hell?

Chapter 6

Who in your community would fill up a house if that person was invited to a party?

What might the owner of the house have thought as he saw the roof being torn up?

Why was the forgiveness of Jesus a surprising twist? (Think this through.)

How do you think the teachers of the law reacted when Jesus healed the man?

Chapter 7

In what ways do you see the war between man and God going on? Is the world getting better or worse in terms of behavior? Cite examples.

Why do so many religions call on people to "go be better"?

How does the way of Jesus differ from these religions? Why is this so controversial?

Chapter 8

Have you ever known someone who died for a cause? What was the cause?

Why is the giving of one's life in war or in saving someone so inspiring?

Why is it amazing that Jesus would die knowing that many would reject Him?

What would you require of others before dying for them?

Chapter 9

What is the greatest or most famous event you have ever witnessed in person?

Which character from chapter 9 best depicts you? Or maybe, used to describe you?

What question would you like to ask God concerning the trial or crucifixion of Jesus?

What has held you back, either now or in the past, from totally believing and following Jesus?

Chapter 10
Which argument for Jesus *not* rising from the dead makes the most sense for you?

Why do people refuse to think through the arguments presented in this chapter?

Who do most people say Jesus was?

Chapter 11
If you had been a follower of Jesus at the time of His arrest, what would you have thought and done?

Would you think that a fisherman could be so eloquent so as to change the minds of three thousand people? Why or why not?

How would the world explain the acts performed by the disciples of Jesus after His resurrection?

Chapter 12
As best you know, explain what someone needs to do in order to follow Jesus.

How has the invitation to follow Jesus been presented to you in the past?

Does the invitation of Jesus seem too good to be true?

Chapter 13
What holds you back from following Jesus completely?

What are the pros and cons of following Jesus?

How does the personal invitation from Jesus affect you?

How to Use This Book

Now that you have completed this book, what comes next?

For yourself

Do some more study. Take a look at our suggestions "For Further Reading" on the following pages, pick up one of the books listed, and continue your search. Study one of these with some friends and hear their ideas.

Attend a church and meet the pastor. Listen to what he says about the Christian life.

Help pass on the story

Give your copy of this book away, or buy another copy to give to a friend or neighbor. Offer to read it with them. Get together to discuss it. Have a weekly coffee meeting and help them work through the book.

Who is someone with whom you have always wanted to share the faith? Buy one for them.

Start a neighborhood or office group. Have a few people on your street or in your office over to read and discuss *Invited*. We included discussion questions to make it easy. We can even arrange a phone conversation between your group and the author at no cost!

For your church

Invited is a resource that is biblically accurate, readable, and challenging and will benefit your entire church family.

Send a copy to your pastor. Ask him how your church could use this short gospel presentation:

Use it as a visitor's gift.

Use it as a small group tool.

Give it to the youth group.

We want to get *Invited* in the hands of as many people as possible and have pricing available so you can afford to give a copy to everyone in your congregation.

We have great discounts for volume purchases in order for you to participate with us in telling the story of Jesus Christ. Contact Randolph McMann at Whitecaps Media by emailing ran@whitecapsmedia.com and our team will make you a deal you cannot refuse!

For Further Reading

To Learn More:

Christian Beliefs: Twenty Basics Every Christian Should Know by Wayne Grudem (Zondervan)

More Than a Carpenter by Josh McDowell (Tyndale House)

The Case for Christ by Lee Strobel (Zondervan)

The Case for Easter by Lee Strobel (Zondervan)

Golf's Sacred Journey: Seven Days at the Links of Utopia by David Cook (Zondervan)

Johnny's U.S. Open: Golf's Sacred Journey 2 (Golf's Sacred Journey Book 2) by David Cook (Sacred Journeys Stories)

More about the Christian Life:

Discipleship Essentials: A Guide to Building Your Life in Christ by Greg Ogden (IVP)

Don't Waste Your Life by John Piper (Crossway)

The Adventure Begins by Kit Sublett (Whitecaps Media)

What Now? Taking the Next Step in Your Walk with Christ by Kit Sublett (Whitecaps Media)

The Four Priorities by Larry Kreider and John Tolson (High Impact Life)

Wholehearted: Three Life Changing Commands of Jesus by Roger Wernette (Whitecaps Media)

ABOUT THE AUTHOR

Originally from Tyler, Texas, Roger Wernette lives in Houston where he serves as the Executive Director of the Houston chapter of The Gathering of Men. He has worked in the banking and financial industry and also on the staff of Young Life. Roger has an undergraduate degree in computer science and a graduate degree in finance from Stephen F. Austin State University in Nacogdoches, Texas, and a master's in theology from Covenant Seminary in St. Louis. He is married to Suzie and they have two sons, Ryan and Chris.

COLOPHON

Cover designed by Stephanie Whitlock Dicken

Book designed and edited by Kit Sublett

Body text is set in Sabon LT Pro, a typeface
originally designed by Jan Tschichold

Printing by Bang Printing, Brainerd, Minnesota

Praise for

WHOLEHEARTED
Three Life-Changing Commands of Jesus

"If you believe, as I do, that God is love, it only makes sense that we should do our best to love God, obey Him, and help others deepen their relationship with Him. In *Wholehearted*, Roger Wernette details these three concepts in a way that is interesting and easy to understand. If you want to grow in your faith, you need to read this book."

—KEN BLANCHARD
coauthor of *The One Minute Manager®*
and *Lead Like Jesus*

"Without clear cut goals, you cannot run a successful business. It is also important to have goals for our Christian life as well. *Wholehearted* sets out some clear goals from which we can all benefit. It tells us where we should be heading with God."

—DRAYTON MCLANE
Former Chairman and CEO, Houston Astros
Chairman, The McLane Group

"I always tried to make my business logical. I wanted all of my people to know our mission and understand what we needed to do next. The Christian life should be simple. Jesus clearly told His followers what they should do. Somewhere down the line, we have made it complicated. Roger brings us back to our roots and I greatly appreciate his effort."

—NORM MILLER
Former Chairman, Interstate Batteries
author of *Beyond the Norm*
co-founder: I Am Second (www.iamsecond.com)

"A practical approach for turbulent times, *Wholehearted* is a straightforward view of discipleship that will challenge and encourage you to develop the most important relationship you can ever have. Read it. Apply it. Grow!"

—SPENCER TILLMAN
CBS Sports
author of *Scoring in the Red Zone: How to Lead Successfully When the Pressure is On*

"This book speaks to everyone who thirsts. We want to love God more. We want to obey God. But how? Within his book are simple, yet powerful, steps to take which enable us to draw on the same Spirit who commands us to love, obey and teach."

—LLOYD M. BENTSEN III
Founder, Houston Christian Foundation